BEYOND INITIAL READING

# Beyond
# Initial Reading -

JOHN POTTS

SCHOCKEN BOOKS · NEW YORK

First published by SCHOCKEN BOOKS 1976

© George Allen & Unwin Ltd. 1976

**Library of Congress Cataloging In Publication Data**

Potts, John, 1924–
 Beyond initial reading.

 Bibliography: p.
 Includes index.
 1. Reading. I. Title.
LB1050.P675  1976    428'.4    75-36499

Manufactured in the United States of America

*For*
*Mona and Mark*

# *Preface*

This book is the result of many years' study of the complex process which we call reading. More specifically, it is the outcome of some four years' research into the development of language and reading skills of 7–11-year-old children. As this study progressed I became increasingly convinced that reading should be regarded as a developmental process in which systematic progression is developed within a structured framework. Reading is also considered to be skilled behaviour and ultimate mastery of the reading process is dependent upon mastering a hierarchy of skills. It would seem logical to conclude from such a broad general view of reading that the many and varied skills which make up the totality should be developed at all stages and levels of education, from the primary school right through to institutions of higher education.

Much of the evidence submitted to the Bullock Committee on reading indicates the need for a fresh approach to the subject. It suggests adopting a wider perspective and sees the development of reading as extending beyond the primary school and into the secondary school.

In writing this book I had four general aims in view:

(i) To increase awareness of the importance of skilled reading both as a study skill and as a means of enjoyment and recreation.

(ii) To show that skilled reading is a necessary adjunct to all academic study.

(iii) To suggest ideas for the systematic development of reading skills across the curriculum.

(iv) To encourage a more active and stimulating approach to reading development and language study in middle and secondary schools.

Whilst the book is primarily aimed at teachers beyond the primary level, the author hopes that many parents and other interested adults might read it with profit. With this in view I have tried to avoid excessive use of technical language.

It would be an impossible task to list by name all those who have contributed to the writing of this book, but I would wish to express my sincere thanks to all my colleagues and friends in many and varied fields of education who have discussed reading problems with me. I am also deeply grateful to the children and students I have been privileged to serve during my teaching career; without their co-operation my own education would have been sadly lacking.

In particular I am indebted to Dr A. Crawford, Senior Lecturer in Psychology at the University of Liverpool, for her unfailing help and support without which this book would never have been written.

The writing of the book has been made easier by the skilful and expert typing of Mrs R. E. Wake, to whom I am very grateful; and by the loyalty and support of my wife throughout my many years of study.

Any shortcomings in the content of the book are my own respon-sibility.

J.P.

*S. Katharine's College*
*Liverpool*
*July 1974*

# Contents

# Introduction

I hope that this book will be a practical and helpful guide to all teachers who are in any way concerned with teaching language and reading in the middle and secondary school. I have tried to suggest the broad outlines of a practical programme by means of which reading skills may be systematically developed. The earlier chapters of the book provide a theoretical and conceptual framework for a reading curriculum.

I firmly believe that the children who would benefit most from a developmental approach to reading are mainly those of average ability who never really learn to use skilled reading as an effective aid to learning. All too often many of these children do not attain their true potential in academic subjects because they fail to capitalise on their skill in reading and do not always realise its importance. This does not generally apply to children who come from homes where books are used both as a source of information and for enjoyment as they are provided with learning experiences at home which reinforce those of the school. On the other hand, those children whose reading ability is so limited that it seriously affects much of their work in school are usually referred to a specialist for the highly specialised teaching which they require.

It is my belief, and this would seem to be borne out by both my own and other research, that many reading problems are inextricably bound up with the inadequate development of linguistic skills generally. Children who are handicapped in this way are unable to manipulate the school situation to their own advantage. This is not to argue that they are linguistically deprived in the accepted sense of the term (see Chapter 8), but rather that the linguistic skills with which such children are most familiar are not the same as those used in the school situation.

Language is so much a part of our everyday lives that we tend to take it very much for granted. In the following pages I have tried to encourage a greater awareness of the marvellous qualities of language as well as some of its mystery. I believe that if this can be transmitted to the children we teach, then reading – which is a linguistic skill – will be less of a problem than it appears to be at present.

# Chapter 1

# Towards Literacy

Many books have been written on the subject of reading in the early stages of the primary school; few have been written with older children predominantly in mind. A great deal of help and guidance is available to the teacher of young children; if she has not received much in the way of instruction from her course of training, she usually has a variety of in-service courses open to her, and even if these are not readily available there is a vast literature on the subject, both in book form and in magazine articles in various educational journals. The teacher of older children is less fortunate. There is little to guide him in the organisation of reading in the classroom, and although specialist help is available if the children have serious reading problems, there is little material which is easily and readily available to help him with those children whose mastery of the skill of reading may be reasonably sound but is still less than perfect. It is hoped that this book will be of value to all who have to deal with this problem.

Reading is a complex skill which is dependent upon the mastery of a number of sub-skills. Most children master the basic sub-skills which are taught in the infant school with some degree of success, but then, for a variety of reasons, they often fail to develop and use these basic skills to the greatest advantage. This is not really surprising since whilst they are young the children are given careful and systematic guidance, but once they have achieved mastery of the basic sub-skills development of competence in using these skills is largely left to chance. The one reading skill which, it may be argued, is developed in many primary schools is that of comprehension, since this is often to be found on the time-table as a special lesson, but teachers tend to forget that different kinds of comprehension skills are developed by the children in the course of tackling problems in diverse subjects across the curriculum. The passages in most comprehension text books contain the wrong kind of information and present too narrow a range of learning experiences for the sound development of a range of skills. Mathematics, science, environmental studies all provide regular and relevant opportunities for the purposeful development of these skills.

It is essential to see reading as a specialised language skill which is a product of a literate society. The close relationship between written and spoken language is too obvious to require elaboration or explanation. But spoken language is directly affected by the environment and many recent studies, for example, those of Crawford (1966)[1], Douglas (1964)[2] and Davie, Butler and Goldstein (1972),[3] have indicated that there could be a relationship between home environment and academic ability as measured by standardised tests of attainment. The author has himself observed that differences may obtain between the academic achievement of children from down-town and related urban areas and those who come from a suburban middle-class environment. These differences are sometimes considerable, especially in cognitive skills. Most children do not start school with a sense of failure, but it is well known by many teachers that by the end of their primary school careers a large number of children are imbued with a sense of failure. Certainly the related tasks of learning and teaching become increasingly difficult in the later stages of the primary school and in the secondary school, by which time many children will have experienced varying degrees of failure in what are commonly regarded as the academic aspects of the curriculum. It would be difficult to isolate a single cause of such failure; the answer to the problem probably lies in a multiplicity of inter-related causes. But the author is convinced that one important causal factor, and it may well be a key factor, is the failure of many of these children to master the reading skills necessary for academic success.

Further, when the skills have been successfully mastered they are not always used as competently and effectively as they might be. Differences in academic ability which are shown by research to obtain between children from a predominantly working-class environment and those from a middle-class background might well be largely accounted for by the tendency of the former group to use language skills ineffectively in the school situation and in particular their slow and often poor development of reading skills. Since reading is one of the basic tools necessary for the successful mastery of formal learning, a lack of ability to use skilled reading effectively increases the prospect of inefficient learning in most other aspects of the curriculum. This is especially so where the learning is dependent upon the child's ability to use sources of information in order to advance his own learning, and this would seem to apply particularly to the later stages of education.

Indeed it might be argued that one of the differences between the child who is academically successful and one who is not lies in the ability of the former to use skilled reading to advantage.

Children who come from homes where reading is positively discouraged, or where there is an apathetic attitude towards books (which may even border on the hostile), make the teacher's task more difficult and possibly more important, since a by-product of such an environment may well be semi-literacy which Jeffreys, as well as others, considers to be a very real danger to a democratic society:

'The . . . reason for the unprecedented power over the human mind is the extreme susceptibility of the human material which is exposed to propaganda and advertisement. The most susceptible victim is the semi-educated person (the well-educated person is forearmed, and the quite uneducated person is comparatively immune); and never before have there been so many semi-educated people in the world – people who are educated enough to be got at, but not educated enough to understand what is being done to them.'[4]

Literacy, which should be the ultimate objective of the reading process, is seen to be of importance at two levels; at the personal level, since to be unable to read and write in a literate society is to be aware of a sense of inadequacy and failure; and at the societal level, as a necessary appurtenance to our democratic society.

There is no easy road to the development of literacy, since it depends upon many factors, but ultimately great responsibility must rest on the schools and particularly on the teachers. It may well be that the sequential development of reading skills which can be utilised at all stages of education could be an important factor. Such skills should not be developed in isolation from the rest of the curriculum but rather that they should be developed across the curriculum. They should be both tools of learning and a means whereby the reader may obtain enjoyment and satisfaction from the printed word. Whilst it is probably correct, therefore, to treat reading as a specialism within the total context of the curriculum, it is wrong to isolate reading as a subject in such a way that it appears to have no relevance to other subjects. Such an approach can easily lead to misconceptions about the reading process as a result of which many children may not be given suffcient guidance about the use of reading as a tool of learning.

Following Harris,[5] the author, in the ensuing pages, classifies reading into two related categories, functional and recreational reading. They are of equal importance but, as will be clear from the text, the objectives are not the same for each category.

Functional reading, that is reading undertaken in order to obtain the information necessary to tackle a specific problem, is of considerable importance. The emphasis here would be on developing the skills required to locate information quickly and efficiently, including the ability to read texts swiftly and with understanding. This aspect of reading is widely applicable to most forms of learning, especially in secondary and higher education.

The importance of functional reading should not relegate recreational reading to a position of secondary importance. Reading is one of the most pleasurable ways of obtaining vicarious experience, and despite television, radio and films, it still has an important role to play in providing a leisure pursuit. Its popularity is evidenced by the wide sale of paperbacks and magazines. But recreational reading, although utilising the same basic skills as functional reading, is a different process, and therefore it should not be treated in the same way as functional reading in the classroom. For example, children should not necessarily be made to read a book for enjoyment in the same way as they would read a problem in mathematics. It is doubtful whether one can teach recreational reading in the way that one can develop functional reading skills in the classroom, but thoughtful guidance could help many more children to be aware of the pleasure to be gained from the printed word.

In the following pages, reading is seen as skilled behaviour which is developed at all stages of education at two levels. Firstly, it is seen as a tool which is essential for learning across the academic curriculum of any school. The skills demanded by the various disciplines tend to take precedence and rightly so, but very often the mastery of these specialised skills depends in the first instance upon efficient and skilled reading. This must be so if the emphasis is to be on guided learning rather than on rote learning and imitation.

Secondly, literature provides the widest and arguably the richest source of imaginative adventures and experiences, but a love of literature, an awareness of its many delights and surprises must be carefully nurtured and cultivated; it cannot be left to chance.

NOTES

1  A. Crawford, Unpublished manuscript of research undertaken into the incidence of reading failure at junior school level in Liverpool (Liverpool, 1966).

2  J. W. B. Douglas, *The Home and the School* (London, MacGibbon & Kee, 1964).

3  R. Davie, N. Butler and H. Goldstein, *From Birth to Seven* (London, Longmans, 1972).

4  M. V. C. Jeffreys, *Personal Values in the Modern World* (London, Penguin, 1960), p. 59.

5  A. J. Harris, *How to Improve Reading Ability* (New Work, Longmans, 1970), 5th edn. This is an invaluable book to which the author, like so many others, is greatly indebted.

# Chapter 2

# Language, Linguistics and Reading

Although it is the intention of the author that this should be essentially a practical book, it is not possible to discuss meaningfully the practicalities of a complex process such as reading without reference to a theoretical and conceptual framework. In the next two chapters, reading will be considered in the context of some of the psychological and sociological aspects of language which have influenced theoretical assumptions underlying the reading process.

## LINGUISTICS AND READING

Language is both a personal and social activity, and because it is so much a part of our everyday lives it is a difficult subject to study objectively. In the following passage Sapir makes implied reference to some of the problems which the student of language has to face and at the same time gives a brief outline of the role of language in society:

'Human beings do not live in the objective world alone, nor alone in the world of social activity as ordinarily understood, but are very much at the mercy of the particular language which has become the medium of expression in their society . . . . The fact of the matter is that the "real world" is to a large extent unconsciously built up on the language habits of the group. . . . We see and hear and otherwise experience very largely as we do because the language habits of our community pre-dispose certain choices of interpretation.'[1]

This passage has implications for the teaching of reading which will be discussed in greater detail in the next chapter.

Since Sapir's early pioneer work there has been a great deal of research in the related fields of linguistics and the psychology of language, and much of this work has been influential in current thinking about many reading problems.

It is not intended to discuss in great detail the arguments about the linguistic approach to language development as exemplified by Chomsky *et al.* and the psychological approach of behaviourist psychologists such as Skinner. But since one cannot discuss reading without reference to the development of language one needs to be aware of these two very different approaches and the implications which each has for the teaching of reading.

Chomsky's basic hypothesis, that we are born with a disposition to acquire language, is at variance with the long-held belief of behaviourist psychologists that language is learned behaviour. The supporters of the linguistic approach believe that what is termed 'universal grammar', meaning the whole system of rules covering the relationships between the phonemic, syntactic and semantic components of a language, is really a way of describing a complex and inborn capacity, an innate idea of language. Such a view may help to explain not only how children learn to speak at all, but how they can learn to speak a variety of mother tongues with equal facility and also how they can learn in spite of such handicaps as deaf and dumb parents or partial deafness.

Chomsky was one of the first to point out that although grammar proposes a set of finite rules which impose a strict discipline on the use of language, nevertheless these rules allow the speaker to generate an infinite variety of sentences. In other words, the speaker has, in principle, the capacity to say new things, to use language creatively.

The work of Chomsky and his colleagues does not, on the surface, appear to be of direct relevance to the classroom situation. But it is largely responsible for the belief, currently held by many reading specialists, that the structure of the language used in basic reading schemes is of considerable importance. In the past, too much emphasis has been placed on the need for a controlled vocabulary in basic readers, and mastery of single words is still widely regarded as the key to successful mastery of the reading process. But whilst word attack and phonic skills are essential to skilled, fluent reading, words themselves often have little meaning outside the context in which they are used. Words such as 'record' or 'present', for example, must be used in a particular context if they are to be correctly interpreted. Chomsky's view that the meaning of a sentence is something more than the sum of the meaning of individual words would seem to imply, if we agree with the argument, that we should be just as concerned about the language structures used in children's readers as we have been in the past about vocabulary.

Lefevre,[2] an American specialist on reading problems and an authority on the relationship between linguistic theory and the teaching of reading, adds support to this view. He insists that to elevate word-learning to a position of highest importance in the teaching of reading is inconsistent with the conception of language as meaningful behaviour. Words contribute to the meanings of phrases and sentences, and the same word may contribute in different ways depending on the meaning of the total structure and the use of different intonation patterns. Central to Lefevre's hypothesis is the idea that:

'A language can only be understood as a structural system capable of generating meaning-bearing patterns. . . . Reading is a language-related process that requires taking in, all at once, patterns of structure and meaning well above the level of the word.'[3]

This problem is well illustrated in a case quoted by Ravenette in his book *Dimensions of Reading Difficulties*:

'A 14-year-old boy attended the child guidance clinic for help with reading, which was about the 8-year level. . . . On one occasion . . . he was reading from a book geared to the older backward readers and was confronted with the following sentence: "Tugboat Annie was liked by all the people in the docks." He got as far as the word "was" and then stopped with a puzzled look. The sentence was re-written, "All the people in the docks liked Tugboat Annie", and this he read unhesitatingly. He was asked about the difficulty and his reply was to the effect that the word "liked" in the original sentence did not seem to make sense, so he did not go on. . . . For this boy it was not that the words could not be read, but that the linguistic form, and therefore the thought form, was unusual.'[4]

Acceptance of Chomsky's approach to language development should not, however, mean rejection of the argument that language is skilled behaviour which has to be learned.[5] The child has to learn his mother tongue and in doing so he develops certain patterns of language behaviour. This emphasis on a skill approach to language is reflected in the view that reading is also skilled behaviour which requires direct and systematic teaching if it is to be fully developed. The relationship between these two kinds of behaviour is clearly stated by Wilkinson:

'The ability to read is largely dependent on the skill in the spoken language the learner already possesses; he has to recognise that visual signs represent the language he knows as sounds. The major reading skills . . . are part of a general linguistic ability that we may characterise as an awareness of the possibilities of language.'[6]

A skill approach to language and reading emphasises the need for a structured programme of study and puts the onus on the teacher to provide systematic learning experiences for the children. This is more likely to provide the practice needed for the development of skilled behaviour than a non-structured approach which relies on incidental learning. In the past, the teaching of language was largely the teaching of grammar, and the structure, particularly in the case of the former, was often so rigid that it was a straitjacket on written expression. As a consequence, 'grammar' has become a dirty word in the teaching of English, particularly in primary schools. But few would deny that a knowledge of grammar is a necessary element of written communication. What is required is a more gradual introduction to grammar and syntax based on an exploration of language and firmly rooted in the spoken word. In other words, there should be greater emphasis on oral language in the classroom with a gradually increasing emphasis on the written word as the child progresses through the various stages of schooling. It is not, therefore, that the teaching of grammar and syntax *per se* is wrong, it is rather the way in which they are often taught in isolation from language in its wider context and without reference to the children's own language.

It would seem to the writer that both the psycho-linguistic and the behaviourist approaches to language have implications of some relevance to the teaching of reading which will be discussed in greater detail in later chapters. But it is worth observing here that both approaches lend support to the arguments put forward in favour of what is called a language-experience approach to reading in which the child's own linguistic skill and experience are utilised to provide a basis for later literacy. This approach has come to be accepted as an important element in the early stages of reading, but its use has been little explored with older children except in cases where a child is referred for special teaching because of serious reading problems. If reading ability is, as Wilkinson states, largely dependent on skill in spoken language it would follow that we could both improve reading skill and provide a wider variety of reading experiences by using the children's own language to a much greater extent than is common in most classrooms.

In this context a fully integrated programme of language studies begins to make sense and can also be seen as a viable proposition. This would, it is hoped, lead to a greater awareness on the part of both teachers and children of the importance of language, and it should also help to develop the creative potential so strongly emphasised by Chomsky but so little recognised in the classroom. Too often we fail to appreciate the child's imaginative and creative use of language, as is well illustrated by the following story.

Some junior school children were set an exercise on synonyms from a certain well known and widely used English text book. One girl wrote in her exercise book the lovely phrase 'as cool as a petal'. When the child's parents were looking through her writing book they noticed that this delightful response had been 'corrected' by the teacher to 'as cool as a cucumber'.

## LANGUAGE, CONCEPT FORMATION AND READING

The relationship known to exist between language and concept formation may also be of some significance to the development of skilled reading. Both Piaget and Vygotsky have expressed the belief that sensorimotor actions as well as words are indispensable to true concept formation. Studying words separately puts the process on a purely verbal plane, which, in Vygotsky's view, is uncharacteristic of the child's thinking. His experimental work on concept formation (Vygotsky, 1934),[8] shows that a concept is formed through an intellectual operation in which all the elementary functions participate in a specific combination. This operation is guided by the use of words as a means of actively focusing attention, of abstracting certain qualities, synthesising them, and symbolising them by a sign. The processes which lead to concept formation develop along two main lines. In the first of these the child unites diverse objects and groups them under a common family name. The second line of development is the formation of 'potential concepts' in which certain common characteristics are singled out, and which has a guiding function in the formation of genuine concepts. The whole complex process is summed up by Luria and Yudovich:

'Language, which incorporates the experience of generations, or, more broadly speaking, of mankind, is included in the process of the child's development from the first months of his life. By naming objects, and so defining their connections and relations, the adult creates new forms of reflection of reality in the child, incomparably deeper and more complex than those which he would have formed through individual experience. The whole process of the transmission of knowledge and the formation of concepts, which is the basic way the adult influences the child, constitutes the central process of the child's intellectual development.'[9]

If the spoken language is closely related to conceptual development, it is reasonable to assume that a relationship exists between conceptualisation and reading. Not only does it help conceptual development, but the reading process itself involves concepts which are often of an abstract nature (Reid, 1966[10] and Downing, 1969).[11] So far, the small amount of research undertaken in this field has concentrated on the earliest stages of reading, but the findings of Reid and Downing would seem to have implications for the later stages also. If these abstract concepts are not fully developed as the child progresses through the developmental stages of intellectual growth, some children are going to have an incomplete conception of what the reading process is all about even when they are quite mature. Reid and Downing both report that for young beginners reading is a mysterious activity to which they come with only the vaguest of expectations, regardless of environmental background. If this is the case, one would expect those children who come from less literate homes to have greater difficulty in coming to terms with this mysterious complex process.

The studies of Morris[12] and others have shown that many of these children never catch up, at least in terms of measured attainment in reading, with their peers from more literate home backgrounds. Such children are the ones who most need help and guidance throughout their primary school careers and probably through much of the secondary school as well. They may not have severe reading problems, but their limitations are a barrier to the full exploitation of the learning experiences provided for them in school.

## LANGUAGE CONSTRAINTS AND READING

Roberts[13] suggests that reading as a linguistic process reflects constraints of language which operate at several levels. For example, the initial letter 't' can only be followed by any of the vowels or a very limited number of consonants; at another level the word 'different' is usually followed by 'from' or 'to', although in practice it is often followed by 'than' in spoken language. Through familiarity with the constraints of language a skilled reader is able to anticipate, within certain defined limits, at any of the following levels: the paragraph, the sentence, the word, the letter-string and the letter. Roberts goes on to claim that without such order reading would be impossible.

It seems reasonable to suppose, therefore, that where the child's verbal language behaviour differs from the printed word, in other words where the verbal constraints do not match the written constraints as in the case of 'different than' instead of 'different from', then some degree of reading difficulty is likely to be experienced. This is one reason why much greater use could and should be made of oral language as an aid to reading at all stages of education, but particularly so with older children where the two aspects of language behaviour have tended to become increasingly divorced from each other.

### READING AS A PSYCHO-LINGUISTIC PROCESS

One of the most scholarly models of reading as a psycho-linguistic process is that devised by Roberts and Lunzer[14] in which they put reading into a clearly defined linguistic framework. Semantically, language is seen to be representational, a system of conventional signs or symbols, comprising units of different size, phonemes, morphemes, strings or phrases, sentences or utterances, and texts. It also has a phonic aspect in that it is a form of behaviour, a complex skill. The sequential arrangement of these units conforms to a system which is the grammar of the language which a child must acquire in learning to speak his mother tongue.

Linguistic behaviour involves concurrent activity at three levels: the representational or semantic, the grammatic or sequential, and the perceptuo-motor or phonic. Since reading is a linguistic skill, all these aspects are as essential to reading as they are to spoken language. Roberts and Lunzer believe that these components are often inadequately taught by the teachers of young children, and that they are not fully realised, if they are realised at all, by the authors of basic primers. Most children supply them from their own considerable store of linguistic skills. If Roberts and Lunzer are correct in their analysis, and there seems no cause to question the validity of their argument, then it would add to the evidence already available that where the child's linguistic experiences differ to any marked extent from those of the teachers and the books which they are using, the chances of such a child having some difficulty in mastering the reading process will be increased.

### READING AS SKILLED BEHAVIOUR

Reading is skilled behaviour in which the reader engages to obtain information. Skilled reading is more than simply the ability to read *per se*. Since the concepts 'skill' and 'skilled behaviour' have been used extensively in our discussion, this is probably an opportune moment to consider them in greater detail.

Bartlett (1947) describes some of the fundamental considerations applicable to any skill in the following passage:

'The good player of a quick ball game, the surgeon conducting an operation, the physician arriving at a clinical decision – in each case there is a flow of signals interpreted to action carried out, back to further signals and on again to more action, up to the culminating point of the achievement of the task. From beginning to end the signals and actions form a series, not just a succession.'[15]

If we analyse this process in greater detail we find that a skill contains three essential elements which must be present before the behaviour can be called skilled. They are:

(i) Anticipation, the ability to use previous experience and evidence in order to construct what is going to happen.
(ii) Automisation, so that the action decided upon as a result of one's anticipation may be carried out swiftly and accurately.
(iii) Analysis of the feedback obtained from perceptual signals.

Where these three elements all combine smoothly, the result is skilled behaviour which enables one to plan a course of action (Herriot).[16]

All these aspects of skilled behaviour are applicable to the reading process. Thus one is able to use past experience in order to anticipate what is coming next in a given text. This is comparatively easy in, for example, nursery rhymes, but it is difficult in unfamiliar texts, for example, the *Cantos* of Ezra Pound. One major difference between a light romantic novel and one by James Joyce, is that in the former one can anticipate with a fair degree of accuracy how the plot is going to unfold, whereas in the latter one can only anticipate a short way ahead, and even this is very difficult in a novel such as *Finnegan's Wake*.

Skilled reading is automatic. It is not skilled if the reader has to stop frequently and think about what he is doing, or if he has to stop and struggle over the pronunciation of words or the meaning of phrases. Thus books which introduce a student to a new subject have to be written in such a way that he can draw upon his past experience in order to master the new material. It is of little use presenting a student who is just starting to study physics with one of Einstein's original papers. He has first to be introduced to the language and concepts of physics and these must be related to his past experience.

Thirdly, the reader must be able to analyse the feedback obtained from the visual perceptual signals on the printed page. This is the essence of some of the basic sub-skills of reading, and failure to master these is a barrier to the development of skilled reading.

Bartlett approached the study of a skill by analysing first the co-ordinations implied by the behaviour in its final form and then seeking to establish the way in which they are acquired. The author has used a similar approach with students as an introduction to the teaching of reading and has found it both more sucessful and more satisfactory than the traditional approach which starts by observing the unskilled performer, that is which starts with the early stages of reading and works upwards. The former approach would seem to be more appropriate to older children, especially those with reading difficulties. But a knowledge of reading as skilled behaviour could well be of help even to good readers, since it would help them to be aware of what is involved in the reading process. They would see, for instance, that one does not necessarily read a novel in the same way that one reads a text book; that a newspaper and a poem are read differently. While many children do eventually develop a variety of reading strategies to suit given situations, it is likely that most will not do so without direct instruction. All teachers, whether they are general subject teachers in the primary school or specialist teachers in the secondary school, could give children more guidance in this respect. In the long term, this would be beneficial to both teachers and pupils since it would help the latter to use library facilities and works of reference such as encyclopedias with greater efficiency in order to advance their own learning. In other words, it would increase their efficiency in abstracting information from a printed page, processing it, and then utilising it in order to solve a given problem.

Roberts and Lunzer explore this point in greater detail. They regard reading as an information processing skill founded on the possession of language. It is seen as a kind of listening using a vi ual instead of an audial input. They regard language itself as a multi-level skill which is developed at three levels: the phonic level is the most basic; the syntactic and semantic levels are ranked as higher-order language skills. These levels are commensurate with the levels of linguistic constraints utilised by the skilled reader in order to obtain and process information from print, as discussed earlier in this chapter.

The higher levels, the semantic and syntactic determinants, remain unchanged and operate to facilitate identification of the input. The phonic aspect of language operates in two ways: firstly, it enables the reader to make use of correspondences between graphemes and phonemes; and secondly, it enables him to identify linguistic information and store it in immediate memory. Skilled reading can be regarded as a hierarchical process of uncertainty reduction in which the key level is the identification of words.[17]

## THE SUB-SKILLS OF READING

Learning to read, then, is primarily a matter of the acquisition of a number of sub-skills which have to be automatised. More complex sub-skills pre-suppose mastery of the earlier, simpler ones.

Some of the earliest work in this field of study was that carried out in the United States of America by Gibson and her associates, notably the experimental work on the critical unit of language for the reading process.[18] Gibson proceeds on the basis that, amongst other things, reading consists of decoding graphic material to the phonemic patterns of spoken language which have already been mastered before reading is begun. The hypothesis advanced is that the task of reading is essentially that of discovering higher-order invariants, the spelling-to-sound correlations. These are constants which are presumably discovered by exposure to both the graphic and the phonemic stimuli at the same time and in different contexts, so that the invariant combinations can be recognised in many different words.

The skilled reader learns to perceive as units the letter patterns conforming to those rules or constraints which enable him to master the reading process. In Britain both Roberts, whose work was discussed earlier, and Merritt have emphasised the need for greater consideration to be given to the sub-skills of reading. Merritt makes the point that a knowledge of these sub-skills can enable teachers to tackle reading problems more systematically and more effectively, since they can provide him with the means to make more accurate observation and diagnosis of reading behaviour than is possible by using such commercially produced tools as the reading tests which are currently available.

## A SIMPLIFIED MODEL OF THE READING PROCESS

Earlier in this chapter we considered very briefly the model of the reading process devised by Roberts and Lunzer. This model, although very informative, is also highly complex and not easy to understand without a sound knowledge of the psychological concepts involved. It might help us to identify some of the problems with greater clarity if we looked at a simple three-stage model of the reading process, viz. :

Stage 1 – pre-reading.[19]
Stage 2 – mastering the basic foundation skills.[20]
Stage 3 – learning how to use reading efficiently and to maximum effectiveness.

We are not here concerned with the first stage, although we should acknowledge its importance to eventual mastery of reading. This book is really about Stage 3 of the model, but for a fuller understanding of the total process we need to consider briefly some of the problems relating to the transition from the second to the third stage. This period of transition from mastering the basic skills to using them in a variety of reading experiences is a critical phase in reading development for many children, although it is seldom recognised as such.

By the time children leave the infant school at seven years of age they are expected to have mastered what Morris calls the basic foundation skills of reading.[21]

At about the age of seven years the teacher has to ensure that the children are able to read with some degree of fluency before they are ready to learn how to use their skill in reading. The transfer from one stage to the other is usually made easily by those children who master the basic skills with little or no difficulty, but this is not so in the case of those children who have experienced difficulty in the early stages. Such children tend to be handicapped from the start and a considerable body of research into their problems indicates that they never really catch up with their more fortunate peers.

The shibboleth of reading aloud to the teacher may well be responsible for the lack of reading ability of many children, as too much emphasis on this particular aspect of reading can actually hinder development. It tends to emphasise one particular reading strategy at the expense of others and, perhaps more importantly, it slows down the rate of reading since the child has to give equal emphasis to every single word in the text. At the stage we are considering, reading aloud should be used by the teacher for diagnostic purposes, that is, she should analyse the mistakes made by the reader and use them to devise programmes designed to increase reading efficiency. Once the child appears to be reading aloud with confidence and understanding he should be presented with a variety of reading experiences designed to encourage the development of differential strategies. Some of these are outlined in greater detail in a later chapter. The teacher should have some idea as to the child's level of ability from observation of his general behaviour. For instance: Does he still use his finger or other aid to guide his reading? Does he stumble over words frequently? Does he show skill in attacking new words? Does he appear confident in his reading ability? To make this observation more objective and systematic, the teacher might draw up an oral reading check list which will also be an aid to more accurate record keeping (see Appendix 1).

When the child appears to be ready to move on from Stage 2 to

Stage 3 of the model the teacher might test his ability by asking him to read a passage silently instead of aloud and then questioning him about what he has read in order to assess his understanding. The author has seldom seen this simple but effective ploy used in the classroom, yet it could be most useful in assessing whether a child is ready to start using his reading skill as an effective aid to study. If the teacher wishes to confirm her own observations of reading behaviour with a standardised test which will assess oral reading ability, speed of reading and comprehension, she might use a test such as the Neale Analysis of Reading Ability (see Appendix 5).

Once the children have successfully completed the transition from Stage 2 to Stage 3 of our model they should be ready to begin a systematic reading programme based upon skilled reading in a wide variety of reading experiences which will develop reading techniques and strategies to meet the many different situations and problems they will have to face as their classroom learning becomes increasingly more academic and discipline based.

### SUMMARY

The aim of this chapter has been to show the relationship between reading and spoken language which exists at many levels. Reading, like language, is skilled behaviour, but whereas it would seem that man has an innate capacity to learn to speak, this is not so with reading. Since the roots of reading lie in spoken language, many of the rules of language are applicable to the reading process and must be applied if reading is to become truly skilled behaviour. Further skilled reading is dependent upon the mastery of a hierarchical structure of sub-skills which can be taught, developed and applied systematically at all stages of education.

In order to use reading most effectively, the reader should be aware of the concepts common to the reading process which will lead to a greater understanding of what reading is and what it can do. The teacher should be able to use this knowledge to devise a reading programme based upon stated objectives and applicable at any given stage of education. This and other points raised in this chapter will be discussed in greater detail in later chapters.

### NOTES

1 Quoted in P. Adams (ed.), *Language in Thinking* (Harmondsworth, Penguin, 1972), p. 123.

2   C. A. Lefevre, *Linguistics and the Teaching of Reading* (Chicago, Chicago Teachers' College, 1962).
3   Ibid., p. 159.
4   A. T. Ravenette, *Dimensions of Reading Difficulties* (Oxford, Pergamon Press, 1968), pp. 42-3.
5   See, for instance, P. Herriot, *An Introduction to the Psychology of Language* (London, Methuen, 1970).
6   A. M. Wilkinson, *The Foundations of Language* (London, Oxford University Press, 1971), p. 202.
7   See D. Moyle, *The Teaching of Reading* (London, Ward Lock Educational, 1968), pp. 96-7 for a brief, critical introduction to this approach.
8   L. S. Vygotsky, *Thought and Language* (Cambridge, Mass., MIT Press, 1962).
9   A. R. Luria and F. La Yudovich, *Speech and the Development of Mental Processes in the Child* (London, Penguin, 1956), p. 22.
10  J. F. Reid, 'Learning to Think about Reading', in *Educational Research*, Vol. 9
11  J. Downing, 'How Children Think about Reading', Distinguished Leader's Address to IRA (Kansas City, 1969), unpublished.
12  J. M. Morris, *Standards and Progress in Reading* (Slough, NFER, 1966).
13  G. R. Roberts, *Reading in Primary Schools* (London, Routledge, 1969). This is an invaluable little book containing many ideas and suggestions for the teaching of reading which would be equally applicable to the secondary school.
14  G. R. Roberts and E. A. Lunzer, 'Reading and Learning to Read', in E. A. Lunzer and J. E. Morris (eds.), *Development in Human Learning* (London, Staples Press, 1968), Vol. 2.
15  F. C. Bartlett, 'The Measurement of Human Skills, in *British Medical Journal* (London, British Medical Association, 1947), Nos. 4510, 4511.
16  P. Herriot, *Language and Teaching* (London; Methuen, 1971).
17  G. R. Roberts and E. A. Lunzer, 'Reading and Learning to Read', in Lunzer and Morris (eds.), op. cit., pp. 220-1.
18  E. J. Gibson *et al.*, 'The Role of Grapheme-Phoneme Correspondence in The Perception of Words' in J. P. de Cecco (ed.), *The Psychology of Language, Thought and Instruction* (New York, Holt, Rinehart & Winston, 1967), p. 186.
19  See J. Taylor, *Reading and Writing in the First School* (London, Unwin Education Books, 1973).
20  Ibid.
21  Morris, op. cit.

# Chapter 3

# Social Aspects of Reading

Reading is essentially a solitary activity, but the reading process is influenced by societal factors and has itself an influence on society.

Where the language structures on the printed page differ from those of the spoken language, the task of learning to read is made more difficult and the possibility of reading failure is increased. This is obvious in the case of immigrant children. It is less obvious, though no less real, when the differences are the result of sub-cultural linguistic variations. It is this aspect of language study which more than any other reflects the influence of sociological thinking.

## LITERACY AND CULTURE

The fact that reading is a skill no longer limited to an educated élite in Western industrialised societies creates problems both for the individual within such a society and for society itself.

Some of the wider societal implications of literacy are suggested by Goody and Watt in their paper on the consequences of literacy. They argue that insufficient weight has been given to the full import of the invention of writing, a product of the urban revolution of the ancient Near East which changed the whole structure of cultural tradition:

'. . . it was only when the simplicity and flexibility of later alphabetic writing made widespread literacy possible that for the first time there began to take concrete shape in the Greek world of the seventh century B.C. a society that was essentially literate and that soon established many of the institutions that became characteristic of all later literate societies.'[1]

With the development of literate societies there grew literary traditions which eventually took over from the older and more established oral traditions. The literary tradition was to set the standards by which academic success is measured in many literate societies. Thus in our society the classical curriculum, which is essentially a product of the literary tradition, is considered to set the standard of excellence to which all formal academic learning should aspire.

But even within a literate culture the transmission of values and attitudes in face-to-face contact is still the primary mode of cultural orientation, and primary group values are all too often alienated from those of the 'higher' literary culture. This may have far reaching consequences for universal education, as Good and Watt imply:

'This introduces another kind of culture conflict, and one which is of cardinal significance for Western civilisation. If . . . we return to the reasons for the relative failure of universal compulsory education to bring about the intellectual, social and political results that James Mill expected, we may well lay a major part of the blame on the gap between the public literate tradition of the school, and the very different, and indeed often directly contradictory private oral traditions of the pupil's family and peer group.'[2]

This conflict is well illustrated by the aims and ideals which lay behind the foundation of the Open University and its actual realisation. Instead of being an institution to enable a working man to graduate, it has become largely a means whereby professional people can obtain extra qualifications.

Such conflict does not exist in non-literate societies. As Mead has pointed out, in primitive societies education is a process by means of which continuity is maintained between parents and children. In more literate societies, particularly those of the industrialised Western world, a function of education is to create discontinuities, as, for example, when it attempts to make the child of illiterate parents literate.

An aspect of literacy that is often overlooked is that as reading and writing are essentially solitary activities it is easier to avoid knowledge in literate societies than it is in those societies which still have a strong oral tradition. Phillpotts make this point with considerable emphasis in her study of Icelandic literature:

'Printing so obviously makes knowledge accessible to all that we are inclined to forget that it also makes knowledge easy to avoid . . . . A shepherd in an Icelandic homestead . . . could not avoid spending his evenings in listening to the kind of literature which interested the farmer.'[4]

It is conceivable that avoidance of learning is more commonplace in schools than we would care to admit, and this could be because of a failure on the part of schools to develop skilled reading systematically as an important study skill. All too often such development is left to chance; but it does not just happen, it must be systematically nurtured through skilled teaching.

LANGUAGE AND CULTURE

It becomes clear that problems arise not simply in the mastery of the reading process, but also out of the values, attitudes and assumptions implicit in the concept of a literate society. Reading is considered to be an essential accomplishment in such a society and mastery of skilled reading is a prerequisite of academic success. Current research indicates that one section of society, the lower socio-economic group, is failing to take full advantage of the educational process. The reasons for this failure are not clearly indicated since it is the result of a number of interrelated factors; but it would seem that a most important factor is the failure of many children in this section of society to master skilled reading. There are strong indications that this reading failure is not unrelated to more general aspects of language development, especially in the early years.

The lower socio-economic social group tends to be less familiar with the essential structure of a literate culture and much more familiar with an oral tradition deeply rooted in folklore. Until quite recently this oral tradition, as exemplified in, for instance, dialect poetry, folk literature and folk music, has tended to be overshadowed by the traditions and scholarship of 'high' literacy. Dialect and idiomatic speech has long been regarded as a barrier to 'getting on in life', and conversely there is an element of suspicion attached to good speech in many working-class communities.

Bernstein noted that such attitudes give rise to culture conflict which manifests itself in many ways in school. For example, many lower working-class children fail to see the need to extend their vocabulary or change their speech habits. Indeed, one might question the need to do so when their language is so often rich in emotion,[5] vivid description and in certain parts of the country rich in humour:

'A public language contains its own aesthetic, a simplicity and directness of expression, emotionally virile, pithy and powerful and a metaphoric range of considerable force and appropriateness. Some examples taken from the schools of this country have a beauty which many writers might well envy. It is a language which symbolises a tradition and a form of social relationship in which the individual is treated as an end, not as a means to a further end. To simply substitute a formal language . . . is to cut off the individual from his traditional relationships and perhaps alienate him from them . . . . It would seem that a change in this mode of language-use involves the whole personality of the individual, the very character of his social relationships, his points of reference, emotional and logical, and his conception of himself.'[6]

From a professional viewpoint it is rather saddening that such a rich store of language experience common to the culture of so many children should be largely untapped by teachers. Greater use of this material in the classroom may help to overcome the conflict of values and attitudes which, it is suggested, is often the result of basing formal education on the values and assumptions implicit in 'higher' literary traditions.

### SOCIO-LINGUISTICS AND READING

Bernstein's work in the field of socio-linguistics has influenced many areas of research in the fields of language and reading, and has opened up new dimensions and provided fresh insights on the whole study of the reading process.

In his early work Bernstein obtained evidence which seemed to show that the lower socio-economic section of the population tends to use a restricted code of language of a kind used in many close-knit communities.* Such a form of language usage does not rely on ex-

*I have used an early nomenclature of linguistic codes in referring to Bernstein's work because this is likely to be more familiar to the reader than later modifications and because the earlier model is better suited to the needs of this particular chapter. The reader should, however, be aware of the later work of Bernstein's research team, which is now fully documented in the two volumes of *Class, Codes and Control*, and the several monographs published in this important series by Routledge and Kegan Paul. In later papers Bernstein makes it quite clear that his original research has moved on into new fields and also that he has himself amended his original views. But despite the fact that on occasions Bernstein has felt obliged to justify his work and clarify his views no one can gainsay the importance of his initial research.
In the USA Bernstein has been influential in much interesting research into the linguistic behaviour of American Negroes, notably that of Labov in his study of the logic of non-standard English, and Baratz and Baratz, who have published several important papers on the wider implications of taking too simplistic a view of the complex relationship between language, learning and culture. For a good introduction to the work of these specialists see *Language in Education*, a source book specially prepared for the Open University course on Language and Learning, which contains several interesting and important papers related to this topic.
The work of Bernstein *et al.* has important implications for the concept of linguistic deprivation. (See Chapter 8.)

tensive verbalisation for the purposes of communication. It tends to contain a high proportion of short commands, simple statements and questions in which the symbolism is descriptive, tangible and concrete. This restricted code differs from the elaborated code which is commonly the basis of the linguistic environment of children from middle-class backgrounds. Bernstein stresses that working-class children are not necessarily inferior to middle-class children in their passive vocabulary (the author's own findings in a small-scale study of the vocabulary of working-class and middle-class junior school children would tend to support this view); it is rather that there are differences in the use of language arising out of a specific context.

It does not necessarily follow that the users of a restricted code will never use elaborated speech variants, but rather that the use of such variants will tend to be infrequent in the socialisation of the child in his family, and therefore they are not likely to be used with ease or fluency by working-class children. Elaborating on this point, Bernstein writes:

'We are discussing two modes of language and the working-class child has learned to respond to only one, and so although he may understand both, he will not differentiate effectively between the two . . . . The working-class child has to translate and thus mediate middle-class language structures through the logically simple language structure of his own class to make it personally meaningful. Where he cannot make this translation he fails to understand and he is left puzzled.'[7]

This different language usage may affect the cognitive processes, albeit indirectly, of many children from working-class areas. The restricted code does not seem to provide such children with the tools of learning which will enable them to succeed in academic education. It is possible that the use of a restricted code helps to make for the slow and often poor development of linguistic skills in general, and reading skills in particular. Certainly in the opinion of the author it is a contributory factor in some forms of reading failure. A language-experience approach to reading which was discussed in the previous chapter may well help to overcome this problem. Such an approach could be built into a reading programme for slow readers at middle and secondary school level, and it might help these children to see more clearly that a relationship exists between the written and the spoken word.

Bernstein's work has further implications for education which, whilst they may not be directly related to language development and the teaching of reading *per se*, nevertheless have an important bearing on these aspects of the curriculum. In a later chapter the implications of Bernstein's research for compensatory education and linguistic deprivation will be considered, but he also makes some pertinent comments about attitudes and motivation.

The language used by the lower working class is essentially one where the stress is on emotive terms employing concrete, visual and descriptive symbolism. Through its use the child learns to respond and make responses to cues which have immediate relevance. But this is at the expense of planning long-term goals which 'tend to be replaced by more general notions of the future in which chance, a friend or relative plays a greater part than the vigorous working out of connections.'[8]

Thus the system of expectancies and the time-span of anticipation of children from the lower working class are shortened. This tends to create preferences and goals different from those which are the norm of schools with their middle-class orientation towards deferred immediate gratification in the interest of long-term goals. The difference in values resulting from this clash of objectives can be a source of tension at the secondary school level.

READING IN THE AGE OF THE MASS MEDIA

Bernstein is one of many sociologists whose work has brought into sharper focus important aspects of the relationship between societal influences and reading. In considering the implications of Bernstein's early work on linguistic problems we have to take into account other social factors, some of which, although they may seem to be peripheral to the central problems of language and reading, are nevertheless of sufficient importance to warrant at least brief consideration.

Developments in media of communication, especially the considerable increase in television broadcasting in recent years, has probably had more influence on reading habits and attitudes than any other single factor. We may choose to ignore McLuhan's philosophical analysis of trends in communication techniques, but it has had a considerable influence on contemporary thinking about the value and purpose of literacy.[9] While a large section of society seems intent on bringing McLuhan's prophetic utterances to fruition, teachers have to convince children that other media, and this includes television, can never wholly replace literature as a means of communication or as a source of knowledge. This is not the place for a lengthy analysis of the pros and cons of McLuhan's argument but we should be aware that if his analysis proves correct, the consequences for society could be drastic.

Whether television stimulates or dulls the imagination is open to argument, and the author is not sufficiently qualified to make a judgement either way. What cannot be disputed is that television viewing seems to have replaced other kinds of activities in which children developed their imaginative powers. Nowadays few children seem to play at seeing pictures in the fire even when they have an open fire to do so. They no longer invent street-corner games, largely because there are few street corners left to play on, but also because television has taken away the incentive to such inventiveness. Even children's toys, with their emphasis on lifelike characteristics, seem to provide little scope for really imaginative play (one would exclude from this category many of the excellent educational toys now on the market and stocked by retailers with a sense of educational awareness).

The school has, consequently, an increasingly important part to play in stimulating imaginative development, and in this particular field literature is of special importance. Not all children respond imaginatively in the same way to a given situation, but there is good reason to believe that the story, if aptly chosen and well told, is a favourite medium with children for imaginative development. Indeed, one could argue that most people of any age enjoy hearing a well-read or well-told and appealing story and will respond to it in their own terms. As far as the school situation is concerned an important problem devolves around the definition of literature. All too often in the past the teacher's ideas as to what is suitable literature for the classroom differ from those of the children, and many teachers reject, for example, books by Enid Blyton and children's comics as suitable classroom material. The Platonic doctrine of the good was relatively easy to uphold in Britain when the only serious competitor was radio broadcasting, for many years under the direction of Lord Reith, a dictatorial figure with very fixed views about what was good and what was bad radio. It is much less so today with the competition from television with its largely visual rather than aural impact. More than ever before, teachers now need to come to terms with those aspects of the children's own culture which impinge upon their formal education. This applies particularly to their linguistic culture and may well involve having second thoughts about what is acceptable literature for children of any given age. This is not to argue that we should always accept the children's standards as our own; it should, perhaps, imply using the children's standards and interests as a base from which to explore a wide range of literature. What we should be seeking is a more active and lively approach not only to literature but to all language studies. English should be one of the most imaginative and lively subjects on the curriculum, not, as it so often is, one of the dullest.

It seems paradoxical that while language seems to be playing an increasingly important role in our everyday affairs, there are such strong factors mitigating its full development. (Here one would include the ubiquitous transistor radio.) These aspects of contemporary society present a great challenge to the professional skills of teachers. But despite the difficulties, we must still aim at developing in children an awareness of the power of language and its related skills both as a tool of learning and as a source of considerable pleasure and enjoyment. A look at some of the examples of children's work in Clegg's book, *The Excitement of Writing*, will show that such an aim is not too idealistic.

SUMMARY

This chapter has tried to place the concept of literacy within a sociological framework. The importance of such a perspective is two-fold. In the first place, the study of language structures leads us to believe that variations in the language behaviour of sub-cultural groups within a society may have a bearing on language and reading development. Secondly, we have become increasingly aware that social groups may have different expectations, values and attitudes which can be important educational determinants.

In literate societies there has been an increasing deviation between literary culture and the folk culture, with the former influencing educational norms, values and attitudes far more than the latter. Since children from lower working-class environments are more familiar with the folk culture, there is a tendency for such children to reject the values and assumptions implicit in formal education because they fail to see its relevance to their particular situation.

In the earliest stages of schooling the child has little awareness of either the differences pertaining to values, or the differences in language usage; but they become increasingly important as he gets older and comes to realise, amongst other things, that language has a personal element which is important to the individual. The work of Bernstein *et al.* provides a theoretical and conceptual framework for these problems.

In the light of the paper by Goody and Watt we perhaps need to look at the total structure of popular education in a literate society. This could have serious and far-reaching consequences for many aspects of education, not least for the aims and purposes of the teaching of reading.

NOTES

1  J. Goody and I. Watt, 'The Consequences of Literacy', in P. P. Giglioli, *Language and Social Context* (Harmondsworth, Penguin, 1972), p. 452.
2  Ibid., p. 342.
3  M. Mead, 'Our Educational Emphasis in Primitive Perspective', in *Journal of American Sociology* (Chicago, University of Chicago Press, 1946), Vol. 48.
4  B. Phillpotts, *Edda and Saga* (London, Butterworth, 1931), pp. 162–3.
5  See, for instance, examples in A. B. Clegg, *The Excitement of Writing* (London, Chatto & Windus, 1965).
6  B. Bernstein, *Class, Codes and Control* (London, Routledge, 1971), Vols 1 and 2, p. 54.
7  Ibid., p. 27.
8  Ibid., p. 32.
9  M. McLuhan, *The Gutenberg Galaxy* (London, Routledge, 1962).
10  See Clegg, op. cit.

# Chapter 4

# Reading in the Middle School

At the infant or first school stage of education the purpose of the reading lesson is fairly clearly defined;[1] the same cannot be said of the reading lesson for children in the middle school age group. There are those teachers who keep the daily or weekly reading lesson on the time-table because it gives the children practice, although just how much reading is done during such periods is an open question. Other teachers no longer set aside a fixed period for reading, preferring instead to integrate it with other aspects of the curriculum. It is hoped that this chapter will provide guidance, or at least food for thought, for all those teachers who have to deal with this difficult subject in the middle school.

By the time children have reached the age of transfer to the middle school most of them should be reading with a reasonable degree of fluency. There will, of course, be those who will require special help, but they are not the main concern of this chapter. Most of the children should have dropped such props as mouthing words and phrases and finger pointing; they should have internalised the reading process and be ready to learn how to use the basic skills with which they have patiently toiled for about three or four years. It is in this field that schools have failed in the past. Once the basic skills have been mastered there has been little or no systematic teaching of the use of these skills.

At this stage of schooling able readers should be ready to appreciate that one can read at different levels and in different ways. Thus adults do not use the same reading techniques when they read a newspaper as they do when reading say a novel or a problem. As teachers we can actively guide children in their reading habits so that they have an early appreciation of this fact.

It might be argued that children will acquire this knowledge with experience. This may well be so, but in the case of the author it was a long time before he developed skilled reading to this extent. Those children who use books regularly may develop such skills as a result of wide and varied experience, but there are those, notably bright children from non-bookish homes, who may never do so unless they are taught how to read at different levels.

In this chapter some ideas for a more systematic but at the same time a more varied approach to the development of skilled reading in the middle school are set out.

## THE CLASSIFICATION OF READING SKILLS

The task of the middle school teacher is to ensure that the children develop effective reading habits, strategies and techniques. In order to do this they have to learn a new range of skills, sometimes termed higher order reading skills to distinguish them from the basic skills. Attempts to classify these skills have resulted in a wide variety of models of the reading process, none of them wholly satisfactory but each contributing something to our knowledge. These higher-order skills are often subsumed under the broad heading of comprehension skills, but this general classification has become too wide to be really satisfactory. We know, for instance, that comprehension takes place at several levels and may be different in kind. For example, a novel and a problem are not comprehended in the same way. Even though both situations are based upon the same basic techniques they each demand different strategies if the outcomes are to be satisfactory to the reader. If we reject the idea that comprehension is a unitary skill we are faced with the difficult task of classifying a systematic range of comprehension skills. We could suggest a very wide range of such skills which would vary from subject to subject across the curriculum, each demanding a range of skills within the subject. But such a model would be so detailed as to be virtually useless.

An interesting and useful new approach to the problem is that of Barrett, who in his model of the reading process suggests five major skill levels: literal comprehension, organisation, inferential comprehension, evaluation and appreciation.[2] Literal and inferential comprehension are not unique to the Barrett model and are commonly regarded as key skills by most authorities on reading.

Literal comprehension is the more obvious and commonly accepted skill area, that is the one to which most teachers refer when they talk about comprehension. In developing these skills we ask the children to find information and ideas explicitly stated in the text, but the questions asked may range from the simple and obvious in the case of young children, to quite complex questions which may be asked of children in the secondary school. Literal comprehension can be developed at two levels using the psychological concepts of recognition and recall which are associated with aspects of memorisation. The simpler of these and most commonly used is recognition where the reader answers questions with the text in front of him and has recourse to it to help him find the right answer. In an exercise of this nature the reader may be asked to recognise from the text such details as the names of characters or places, the main ideas of the text or a sequence of events. The list could be extended but there are sufficient examples here for the reader to obtain a good idea of the kinds of tasks set in this particular exercise.

We can ask the reader to find information of the kind suggested above without recourse to the text when answering questions, indeed the teacher may ask for the information after a considerable time lapse. In tasks of this nature we call upon a different aspect of memorisation, what the psychologist terms recall. This kind of comprehension could, possibly should, be developed gradually but it is often too difficult for slow children except on a very limited scale. Except with the brightest children it would seem to have more application in the secondary school than in the middle school.

Although inferential skills have long been acknowledged by many teachers their full importance has only quite recently been recognised. Whilst it may seem obvious to ask children what is explicitly stated in a text, it is less so to ask them what may be implied. In developing inferential skills we are encouraging the reader to read critically and to analyse carefully what he has read. He is asked to use the information which he obtains from the text and his own experiences and ideas in order to make inferences about the content of a text. As in literal comprehension skills the tasks can be classified. The reader might be asked to infer what supporting details or additional data the author of a given text or passage might use to make it either more informative or more interesting. Or he might be asked to summarise the main idea or thesis of a text where this is not explicit. These kinds of skills are often tested in examination situations at secondary school level. A skill sometimes used by teachers in relation to written work in the junior school and which is classified as an inferential skill is that of commenting on a sequence of events. For instance, the teacher may outline an uncompleted sequence of events in a story and ask the children to complete it. Under this same heading of inferential skills a reader may be asked to infer character traits on the basis of clues given by the author of a text. The author has used this approach with some success in both oral and written composition work with 10- and 11-year-old children, in fact he has developed this particular area of skills with top junior school children in class discussion and written work rather than specifically in reading comprehension.

It will be seen then that even a simplified model of the reading process implies developing deeper and more subtle levels of understanding as the reader becomes more skilled. It is sadly true that too many children, and adults too for that matter, never progress beyond the stage of recognition in literal comprehension, even though inferential skills are becoming increasingly important. All too often what is left out of a text can be more important than what is included in texts such as statements to the press or official reports. This also applies to what we commonly regard as literature, as readers of the short stories of Jorge Luis Borges for example, will know.

The importance of a skill approach to reading has recently been recognised by the Schools Council which has set up two research programmes to study a structured approach to the teaching of reading at the middle school age ranges. At Manchester, Mrs V. Southgate Booth is directing a programme aimed at studying all school activities of 7- to 9-year-old children which are in any way connected with the development and use of reading skills. Another similar programme is being undertaken with older children under the direction of Professor E. A. Lunzer and W. K. Gardner at Nottingham. The outcomes of these two projects, due in 1976, should be most interesting and, it is hoped, helpful to teachers.

## AIDS TO THE DEVELOPMENT OF READING SKILLS

Teachers wishing to devise programmes to develop reading skills but lacking the expertise or the time or both might usefully explore some of the commercial aids which are now on the market. Amongst the foremost of these are the various reading laboratories which were first introduced in the mid-1950s and which aim at developing reading skills to a very high level. Reading laboratories are designed for individual learning situations, each child starting from his existing level of competence. The child works on small self-corrected assignments, leaving the teacher free to act as what Moyle terms 'programme consultant' and 'curriculum planner'.[3] While the reading laboratories require the minimum of direct supervision they do not absolve the teacher from all responsibility, as is implied by Moyle's suggested roles. He has to be familiar with the kits and must know what skills are practised at each stage in the laboratory. This is essential if the child is to learn how to use the skills outside the laboratory situation, since we cannot be certain that the child will make such a transfer automatically. It should perhaps be emphasised that reading laboratories, although ideally suited, if correctly used, to both the middle and secondary school, only provide a limited range of reading experiences; they are intended to supplement, not supplant, book reading. Dr Parker, who introduced the SRA reading laboratories,[4] pioneers in the field, suggests that the best results are obtained when they are used as 'booster' programmes for one term in three, and the limited research which has been carried out in this country, for instance by Moyle (1966) and Pont (1966),[5] would seem to support this view.

The most comprehensive laboratory approach to reading is provided by the SRA reading laboratories. These were introduced into Britain from the USA and the early ones tended to reflect aspects of American society, but the later ones have been adapted to suit British needs. The first British attempt at developing a reading laboratory was the *Reading Workshop* published by Ward Lock,[6] which is not so comprehensive as the SRA laboratories and does not cover such a wide age range. The systematic development of reading skills is not as clearly defined in the *Workshop* as in the SRA laboratories. The latest British venture, the *Language Centre*[7] seems to come closer to the American model. It is described as a comprehensive language arts programme and is designed initially to cover the primary school age range.

The laboratory approach to the development of reading skills is now used in many primary schools and the author has observed that most children learn to use them effectively in quite a short space of time and, perhaps of greater importance, seem to enjoy using them.

Reading systems are the most recent development in the teaching of reading. The most comprehensive of these is that published by Scott Foresman, an American publishing house.[8] This is designed to cover the whole of the primary school age range and is remarkable for the thoroughness with which it provides for skill development from the pre-reading stage.

The teacher has, therefore, quite a wide range of aids to assist in the development of reading skills, but these are of little use unless they are backed up by skilled teaching. In the last analysis, success in the classroom is dependent upon the skill of the teacher and the most sophisticated aids will not alter this situation.

THE QUALITIES OF READING EXPERIENCES

In adopting a skill approach there is the danger of fragmenting the reading process to such an extent that the totality, which is something greater than the sum of all the constituent parts, becomes unidentifiable. We should never lose sight of the ultimate goal of the process, which is the development of literacy however this is defined.

Even if we could break down the process into an agreed body of knowledge and skills we should still have to take account of such aspects as the qualities of reading experiences. Reading, in the widest sense of the term, refers not just to the skills used by the reader, but also to the effect the material may have on him. This may be a vicarious physical experience if we are reading, say, a James Bond novel, or an emotional experience arising from our response to a passage in which the writer creates what is to the reader a strong sense of drama. In addition to these aspects of reading, there is also a cognitive experience which affects us all as we comprehend the material we are reading at different levels of understanding.

Merritt[9] argues, and few would care to disagree with him, that performing skills alone without the accompanying experiences cannot be regarded as reading in the true sense of the term. The total process includes the skills performed in responding to the printed text and the whole range of experiences which result from exercising these skills. Teachers need to take account of this aspect of the reading process when devising a programme of reading experiences for their children. The emotive and physical experiential aspects would obviously be of paramount importance in considering the suitability of children's literature *qua* literature, but it is of importance in all aspects of reading. If the experiences we provide are unsatisfactory for the children we teach, we can hardly expect them to develop what we would regard as satisfactory reading habits.

## READABILITY

In trying to provide suitable reading experiences for children many teachers find difficulty in assessing whether a book is suitable for a given child in terms of language structure, vocabulary, the author's style and other important factors. Where the children are using a basic reading scheme the problem is less acute because these readers are usually carefully graded and the teacher is able to select books of about the right order of difficulty by referring to the information supplied by the publishers. Many of the excellent series of supplementary readers for use at primary school level are also similarly graded. The same is not true of most text books or of the many excellent novels and reference books which are now published for children. Thus the problem applies more to the age range of 9 to 14 years, the stage when the children should be enjoying a wide range of reading experiences in order to develop their skills. To overcome the problem we need a measure of assessment of what is called the 'readability' of a book.

Readability has been defined by Dale and Chall in the following terms:

'In the broadest sense, readability is the sum total (including inter-actions) of all those elements within a given piece of printed material that affects the success which a group of readers have with it. The success is the extent to which they understand it, read it at optimum speed and find it interesting.'[10]

Briefly we may define three areas of importance in assessing readability: legibility, interest, and ease of understanding. Since Gilliland[11] revived interest in the concept of readability in Britain in 1968 there have been several interesting and useful developments in this field, particularly in the development and use of cloze procedure. The word 'cloze' is derived from the concept 'clozure' which is applied by gestalt psychologists to the tendency to complete a familiar but incomplete pattern by mentally filling the gaps. The principle is familiar enough in spatial patterns, for example if we see a broken square we tend to complete it, but it can also be applied to both language and music. Thus, if one hears a few bars of a very familiar melody one tends to complete the musical phrase; in language one would complete a familiar but unfinished verse if given sufficient clues to recognise it. (This ploy was used to good effect by Frankie Howerd in a popular television series called *Up Pompeii.*)

Taylor[12] defines the cloze unit as it applies to language as 'any single occurrence of a successful attempt to reproduce accurately a part deleted from a "message" [any language product] by deciding from the text that remains what the missing part should be'. In using cloze procedure then, the reader is given texts which are incomplete because a selection of words has been omitted. The deletions may be made on the basis of every 'n'th word or they may be made on a lexical basis, that is restricted to certain grammatical forms such as nouns, verbs or adjectives. A commonly accepted rate of deletion for adults is every fifth word of a text, but with younger children a deletion rate of one word in ten may be more advisable.

We could use this procedure to assess the readability of books by having selected passages from each book reproduced with words deleted on the basis suggested above depending upon the age of the children. The reader should complete the passage by replacing the blanks in the text with a correct response. In scoring the exercise one mark is given for each correct response and the total score should indicate the suitability of the text for the reader. The limited research on this aspect of the problem would seem to indicate that a score below the 40 per cent level would imply that the material is too difficult for the reader.

This is only a brief account of a process which is discussed very fully in Gilliland's book, *Readability*, but it does show the value of readability as a concept and the cloze procedure as an aid to the more objective assessment of the suitability of reading material.

RECREATIONAL READING

As the title implies, recreational reading is essentially reading for pleasure. This is a very simple definition, but it will serve for the purposes of our discussion. The set reading lesson usually has an emphasis on recreational reading and as it is usually organised in most schools one must have doubts as to whether it really serves much purpose for many children. (It is worth recalling Phillpotts's comments about the ease with which one can avoid knowledge in literate societies, see Chapter 3, page 34.)

The following suggestions, although not very original, indicate how more variety and greater pupil involvement may be introduced into the reading lesson.

*The classroom environment*

It goes without saying that there should be a variety of well-produced books attractively displayed in the classroom. But unfortunately this aspect of reading is often relegated to a very low place in the order of things. The usual jumble of books tucked away in a corner of the classroom is hardly likely to stimulate the children to pick up the books and spend a few minutes browsing through them. Granted that good display is a skill not possessed by all teachers, but there is usually at least one teacher on a school staff who has this gift and it would certainly be put to good use in keeping books attractively displayed. The local library staff may be willing to help in this respect and put on special displays. Attractive book displays can be centred upon topics of interest, television series and the like. These should be changed regularly, half a term is usually quite long enough for a classroom display if it is to retain its effectiveness for the children. Centralised book displays for the whole school are a much bigger venture requiring careful thought and preparation and may be more effectively planned on a termly basis. Whether such displays are mounted in the classroom, the library or the entrance to the school they should have one objective, namely to encourage the children to explore books.

A good reading environment is not a substitute for sound teaching, but it should be an important element in any reading programme. The teacher, by giving thought to book display, indicates to the children that books are important and are there to be used, enjoyed and respected. Unfortunately books, like language, tend to be taken too much for granted. A stimulating environment will help to overcome this.

## *The organisation of the reading lesson*

It is doubtful whether there is much to be gained from the reading period where the children are made to sit quietly with a book in front of them. The good readers who enjoy books will benefit, but they probably read avidly both inside and outside the classroom, and they are usually in a minority. Other children may well sit quietly and go through the motions of reading, but it is very difficult for a teacher to evaluate just how much reading is done during such a period. This is not to argue that periods of silent reading should be dispensed with altogether, simply that the cause of reading and literacy would be better served by an approach which offers more variety. There is scope for greater active participation on the part of the children during periods when they explore books and literature. Such an approach would offer the children guidance which many of them need when faced with such a wide variety of choice as is afforded by books. For example, the children might be given guidance about plot and character through discussion. The teacher might take a short story and discuss with the class the way in which the writer introduces it, how the plot is developed, and how he outlines the characters The author has used this approach successfully with 10- and 11-year-old children and found some of the short stories of O'Henry and W. W. Jacobs ideal for such a purpose. As a follow-up, the children tried their hand at writing short stories with some degree of success. They needed help in selecting a suitable situation and this was given through class discussion. As an alternative to this individual approach to short-story writing, groups of children might work together on outlining the plot and characters of a story, first recording the story on tape and then writing it out. Recording on tape would enable them to record their ideas quickly and also to make any necessary amendments to the story after hearing it read through.

If the teacher cannot find suitable short stories he might précis a novel for the purpose of discussing plot and character; the children could then decide whether they would like the teacher to read the book as a serial.

If such teaching as is suggested above is to be alive and meaning-ful to the children, it does require that the teacher be prepared to explore books himself. All too often the teacher's choice is a repeti-tion of what he was told were good books for children when he was in training. This is not to imply that the accepted classics of children's literature are no longer suitable, indeed it is rather sad that the Greek and Norse legends no longer seem to be popular with teachers although they still appear to be favourites with children. But today there is a great variety of books available for younger readers and there are some interesting modern authors whose work is of such a high standard that it deserves to be explored. If the teacher is not able to explore literature himself he might consider using the services of the public library. In many of these there is usually at least one librarian on the staff with a sound knowledge of literature for younger readers, and this expertise could well be put to more effective use by schools. Co-operation with specialist departments in secondary schools, colleges of education and university departments of educa-tion might also open new sources of information to the teacher and should certainly be explored.

An interesting piece of experimental work which may help to develop a wider interest in books is being carried out in the East Riding of Yorkshire under the auspices of the Schools Council.[13]* Children, teachers, parents and the library service are all involved in this venture. A group of heads, disappointed at the response of children to new books with which school libraries had been stocked, but aware of the difficult problem of keeping abreast with new publi-cations, discussed the problem with the County Children's Librarian, who was also concerned about the books selected by children. As a result of their concern and discussion of the problem, reading groups have been set up in certain schools to consider new books as they are published. The librarian acts as a guide to selection and books are read by teachers to children and by groups of parents and teachers. Comments are made on the books and copies of these are sent to

*The Schools Council is a semi-official, non-profit-making body which has been responsible for a great deal of curriculum innovation in Britain during the last decade or so.

schools. In this way a group of schools is keeping abreast of books as they are published, and have a reliable indicator as to whether they are popular or unpopular with the children. The idea of co-operating with the public library service and involving parents in choosing books is one which could certainly be adapted and extended.

## The keeping of records

Record keeping may not seem to be an essential part of a recreational reading programme, but it is important to keep a record (a) in order to evaluate the programme, and (b) in order to build up an anthology of books.

Too often in the past children have been asked to write an account of a book which they have read and this has been the extent of the record keeping. But this task, apart from being quite difficult in itself, may well take the gilt off the gingerbread; certainly it is unlikely to encourage children's reading. Other methods of record keeping need to be explored.

All children should keep their own records of books which they have read and try to evaluate them, even if it is only on a very simple scale. They might be encouraged to comment in greater detail on books which they have very much enjoyed or alternatively on any which they have positively disliked. The teacher would find it useful to keep a record of such comments as they can be a source of information for discussions about books, and comments by children can often be more revealing and more relevant than the comments of critics.

As a change from written accounts the children might tape-record their opinions about a book. If the taped comment is good it could then be written out to keep a permanent record. The tape itself could be used to introduce a discussion of either this particular book or books of a similar kind, for instance comments on the novel *Shane* could lead to a discussion of cowboy stories, a topic which has limitless possibilities.

The relationship between writer and reader could be explored more deeply than has sometimes been the case in the past. The author has used drama as a means of exploring this relationship and has found this to be successful with children of middle school age. A group of children might be asked or elect themselves to read a particular book and then dramatise certain key parts of it. (Dramatisation of the whole of a fairly lengthy novel might be rather difficult.) The dramatisation could again be used to stimulate class discussion and it would also give the teacher an insight into how the children concerned had reacted to the plot and characters in the book.

Teachers themselves should keep their own list of popular and unpopular books, much as many of them keep their own anthology of poems. Interest might be increased if, apart from book displays, the children's own critiques of books were mounted in magazine form so that they could be used by all the children in a class or a school. Ideally there should be two sets of such comments, those of the children themselves and book reviews from newspapers and magazines, many of which carry monthly reviews of new books for younger readers. Further interest might be added by selecting a book of the month along the lines of selection of popular records. The local library and the local bookshop would probably be prepared to co-operate in such a venture.

For too long books have been paradoxically both taken for granted and regarded as being rather special in school. We should endeavour to put them firmly within the culture pattern of the children.

## A recreational reading programme

Whilst it may not be desirable to be too systematic in developing recreational reading, it is possible, nevertheless, that a planned reading programme is more likely to improve the children's attitude towards reading for enjoyment. The following objectives (based on Harris)[14] are suggested as a framework for a reading programme which should encourage children to be more selective and more adventurous in their choice of reading material.

(1) *The development of a liking for reading as a leisure-time activity.* In the development of recreational reading the realisation that reading can be an enjoyable recreation should be a major objective. But children cannot be made to enjoy reading, so enjoyment must be developed as a result of voluntary effort. This implies encouragement and guidance rather than direction. By providing a varied approach to reading in which the children play an active rather than a passive part, the teacher is more likely to encourage a larger number of children to explore books for sheer enjoyment than is the case if they are simply left to fend for themselves. This is not to argue that all children need help. Those who are used to choosing books from a library and who read for pleasure regularly may resent any interference with their freedom to choose their own reading matter. But those who do little reading could well benefit from help and guidance.

(2) *The development of increasing maturity, variety and refinement in choice of reading matter*. This is necessary if the children's reading is really going to develop. The emphasis on exploration is an attempt to meet this objective. A wider knowledge of children's books which should result from co-operation with teachers in other schools and with the library service would help the teacher to achieve this objective.

(3) *The development of a liking for oral reading as a means of entertainment*. The story is one of the oldest and most popular forms of entertainment and its continuing popularity is evidenced in many ways, for instance the serialisation of books on the radio, the use of story in folk music and poetry. All children enjoy a good story when it is well read and when it appeals to their interest. Today the teacher has a much wider choice of material than he had in the past but book reviews, book programmes on television and radio can offer guidance about the suitability of books for any given age group. The teacher should be prepared to discuss books with children before deciding whether to read a certain book. He could, for example, tape-record sections of the book and discuss these with the children to assess their reaction. This would involve the children much more in deciding whether to adopt a book for serialisation. It would also give the teacher the opportunity to evaluate his own strengths and weaknesses as a story-teller, and prevent a hit-or-miss approach in the selection of suitable material.

*The skills of recreational reading*

There are certain skills which, if developed, will add to the pleasure to be obtained from reading and which are necessary if the reading is to become really skilled. The author does not consider the following list to be definitive but hopes that it will provide some guidance for colleagues.

(1) *The ability to understand a sequence of events*. The children's own writing could be used as an aid to facilitate this skill. Their stories will show whether they can develop a sequence of events from a beginning to a conclusion. In this they may need considerable help, especially in the early stages. The old exercise of providing children with a story told in a series of pictures is a useful starting-point but this should be developed up to the stage where the children are writing their own stories. Those children who find writing difficult could narrate the story and tape-record it before committing

themselves to paper. As an alternative exercise in developing this skill, the children might be asked to illustrate a story in a series of pictures depicting key incidents and introducing the main characters.

(2) *The ability to grasp the organisation of an author's plan or the plot of a story.* Often when children are asked to write about books which they have read they attempt, albeit unwittingly, the very difficult task of making a précis, and in so doing they are not always successful in commenting on key incidents. Questions about the plot or the characters in a story would give the problem greater definition and thus make a difficult task easier, particularly for those children who have not developed skill in writing reports. Book reviews would provide useful models of how to comment on books, bringing out essential details without spoiling the story for the potential reader.

(3) *The ability to evaluate a book or a story.* The questions suggested in (2) above would also be of value in helping to cultivate this skill. Children could more actively discuss books than has been the case in the past. There is no good reason why two children, one of whom likes a particular book or author and one of whom does not, should not state their case to a class or group of children. Many of the other activities suggested in this chapter will help to develop skill in evaluation. It is perhaps worth mentioning that evaluation at this level will tend to be subjective; there are no absolute criteria by which one can judge a book, but encouraging children to talk about their choice of books and to think about the reasons for their choice should lead to a consideration of such aspects of writing as style at the secondary school stage.

The suggestions outlined above should lead to a more mature understanding of the enjoyment to be obtained from reading and a discriminatory approach to reading for pleasure. Many schools still seem to be under the spell of 'silent' reading. Of course there is a place for this; but equally children should be encouraged to share their enjoyment and their enthusiasm with their friends.

FUNCTIONAL READING

In a literate society skilled and efficient reading is of fundamental importance in almost all aspects of formal learning, but many children only acquire skilled reading by chance.

In his contact with students from a wide variety of backgrounds the author has often had to devote time to basic study skills, including the use of reading skills, in order to promote effective learning. When faced with a new subject students really do become aware of their limitations in reading. Their deficiencies would not be so pronounced if reading skills were taught systematically in schools.

*The reading specialist in the middle school*

Since it would be expected at this stage of education that at least some teachers would undertake specialist work within their disciplines, it is unlikely that all teachers in the middle school will be experts on reading. But the writer firmly believes that each school should have at least one teacher on the staff with some expertise in this field. Ideally the 'specialist' teacher would have at least a special interest in reading problems, but he should also be familiar with wider aspects of language teaching. It would seem, therefore, that apart from interest, the teacher should have some specialist knowledge of the teaching of English. Wide experience would probably be a better qualification than narrow specialism at the middle school stage. This is, of course, a much wider brief than the more usual one of a specialist teacher for remedial work. Whilst the specialist may or may not undertake such work, he should certainly be able to advise colleagues on the development of language and on the teaching of reading, especially on how they can best foster reading skills in the context of their own particular field of study. More often than not, problems are posed in such subjects as mathematics without any real thought given to the reading skills demanded of the child before he can tackle the problem. The reading specialist should be able to devise a reading programme by means of which comprehension skills are systematically taught and developed across the curriculum.

*A systematic reading programme*

A systematic programme for the development of basic comprehension skills should have two general aims:

(i) to develop an awareness on the part of the child that the written word presents information at several levels;
(ii) to develop increasing accuracy and precision in retrieving information from the printed page.

A programme designed to achieve these aims might be devised along the following lines.

Initially when children are asked to obtain information from sources such as, for example, Ladybird reference books, they might be referred to a specific book, page and even paragraph. As proficiency is developed in using these simple reference books, children can be referred to more advanced books in order to obtain required information and the amount of guidance decreased, for example to the book title and chapter. The task of finding information should be gradually increased in difficulty as the children are encouraged to use tables of content and indexes. Such a programme should lay the foundations for the more advanced skills which the children will need at secondary school and to which reference is made in the following chapter. The children themselves should be encouraged to note with precision and accuracy the sources of information which they have used in order to solve a given problem.

*Skill objectives for a functional reading programme (after Harris)*

(1) *The ability to grasp meaning at increased levels of difficulty, for instance sentence, paragraph, chapter.* This can be developed by thoughtful preparation of problems related to the ability of the children. For instance, they could be asked to select key words, or a key phrase from a paragraph at a fairly elementary level, whilst older children could précis longer passages in order to extract from them essential information.

(2) *The ability to follow directions accurately.* This is a key skill which might perhaps be better developed aurally before the children follow written directions. The development of this skill imposes on the teacher responsibility for making sure that any instructions, whether they be written on work-cards or recorded on tape, are clear and concise.

(3) *The ability to find answers to specific questions.* This is a skill which can be developed in a variety of learning situations. Successful development will largely depend not only on the kind of question asked but also on the provision of a good supply of reference books.

(4) *The ability to note and recall facts.* This skill, which is so essential in more advanced learning, is all too often neglected in schools. Children do need guidance in how to set out notes so that the information which they contain can be recalled quickly and easily. Too often one finds that even students in higher education do not possess this skill, and find note-making, as opposed to note-taking, very difficult. This problem could be minimised if this particular skill were more systematically developed in the classroom.

*Specific reading skills applicable to functional reading in the middle school*

The following specific skills are directly related to the skill objectives and will in many instances advance their achievement:

(a) The ability to use an index.
(b) The ability to use a table of contents.
(c) The ability to use a dictionary.
(d) The ability to locate information in an encyclopedia.

In addition, children at this stage of schooling, particularly at the upper levels, should start to develop the use of methodical reading such as scanning when searching for information. This skill is used by most children at some time in their reading; discussion and practice can make it an efficient method of ascertaining the content of a book or a chapter.

The skills outlined above can be developed in all those areas of the curriculum of any school where children have to use their skill in reading in order to advance their knowledge. In the long term such a programme would benefit all children and not just those who will go on to further or higher education. Indeed, it is possible that if these skills were developed systematically in schools more children could benefit from formal education as they would be provided with tools of learning which many children at present lack.

## SOME WIDER ASPECTS OF LANGUAGE STUDY IN THE MIDDLE SCHOOL

Topic work in whatever form it is undertaken provides a useful opportunity for the wider exploration of language. The author has used the following suggestions with some degree of success in teaching children aged between 9 and 12 years of age.

If topic work is to have any value it should, amongst other things, assist the development of concepts related to the disciplines covered by the topics and enlarge the children's vocabulary. It should not be too difficult in preparing topics to draw up lists of key words and phrases to which the children will be introduced and which will relate directly to the new material being learned. The words can be used for vocabulary work and for spelling. The children could, for example, note them in special vocabulary books, find out what they mean, use them in meaningful sentences or passages, and possibly find out the derivation of particular words or prefixes such as 'sub' and 'aqua'. They can be tested on their knowledge in a variety of ways. They might, for example, be encouraged to make up a cross-word puzzle using all or some of the words; devising suitable clues is in itself a difficult but challenging and interesting exercise. The selected words might be used in a piece of dictation which is also a summary of the work done in the topic.

The author is well aware that dictation is no longer fashionable, but, like so many other educational exercises which have fallen from grace in the past few years, it is not so much the task itself as its thoughtless use which should be criticised. Occasional dictation has value on at least two counts. In the first place it has some value as a listening skill and it can also serve to test skill at spelling. The value of such an exercise is enhanced if it is related to work which has been undertaken by the children in the course of their studies, as suggested above.

At the upper end of the middle school age range there is no reason why the children should not develop their own written shorthand for personal notes as many adults do, but they must realise that when written language is used to communicate information to someone other than the writer it must obey certain rules which include punctu-ation and spelling. There is a need for direct and purposeful language teaching related to learning situations which provide both a rationale and an incentive for good, accurate use of language. A more struc-tured approach to language study such as that outlined above would lead to improved standards in both spoken and written English. Greater appreciation of the importance of language and knowledge of its use can only be of benefit both to the individual and in the long term to society.


## SUMMARY

Children should appreciate that reading is undertaken at different levels and for various purposes. If reading is intended as a recre-ational activity the emphasis should be on enjoyment. This is more likely to be cultivated if there is a more active approach to the teach-ing of reading in the middle school in which the children and teachers together participate in exploring books and literature.

The emphasis in functional reading should be on the development of special skills, especially more advanced comprehension skills and information retrieval skills. These should be developed within a reading programme which utilises many aspects of the curriculum. In this way the reading has a purpose and the learning is more likely to be positively reinforced by relevant usage.

The use of topics in school also provides opportunities for a more structured approach to language study, which should lead to improved standards in both spoken and written English.

## NOTES

1  See, for instance, J. Taylor, *Reading and Writing in the First School* (London, Unwin Education Books, 1973).
2  T. C. Barrett, 'Taxonomy of the Cognitive and Affective Dimensions of Reading Comprehension', in A. Melnik and J. Merritt (eds), *Reading Today and Tomorrow* (London, University of London Press for the Open University, 1973), pp. 55–60.
3  D. Moyle and L. M. Moyle, *Modern Innovations in the Teaching of Reading* (London, University of London Press, 1970).
4  SRA Reading Laboratories (Henley-on-Thames, Science Research Associates).
5  Moyle and Moyle, op. cit.
6  *Reading Workshop* (London, Ward Lock Educational).
7  Language Centres (Cardiff, Drake Educational Associates).
8  Scott Foresman Reading Systems (Brighton, Scott Foresman, 1972).
9  The author is indebted to an excellent unit prepared for the Open University Course on Reading Development by Professor John Merritt. The reader will find much of value in these units which are available from the Open University at Milton Keynes.
10 E. Dale and J. S. Chall, 'A Formula for Predicting Readability', in *Educational Research Bulletin*, No. 27 (1948), pp. 11–12.
11 J. Gilliland, *Readability* (London, University of London Press, 1972).
12 W. L. Taylor, 'Cloze Procedure: A New Tool for Measuring Readability', in *Journalism Quarterly*, Vol. 30 (1953), pp. 415–33.
13 See 'Dialogue', in *Schools Council Newsletter*, No. 15 (Autumn 1973).
14 A. J. Harris, *How to Increase Reading Ability* (New York, Longmans, 1970), 5th edn.

*Chapter 5*

# Reading in the Secondary School

Because of the greater fragmentation of the curriculum and the emphasis on a specialist approach to subjects, the teaching of reading presents greater problems in the secondary school than it does in the middle school. There seems to be an assumption that at this stage of education special instruction in reading is only needed by those students who have reading problems which interfere with their ability to learn. The author's work with students in higher and further education indicates weaknesses, not only in reading habits and attitudes, which are serious enough in themselves, but also in the application of skilled reading to academic study. These strictures probably apply to many students in higher education, but they are usually unaware of any deficiency in the application of reading skills. Most have demonstrated in the selection procedures that they have reading ability, but the application of that ability to real learning situations is seldom examined with any degree of thoroughness. It is probably true to say that only a minority of students entering higher education are what one might term book lovers, and yet most of these students are going to enter professions where they will be concerned with books of one kind or another for most of their working lives.

The most serious aspect of the problem is not simply the general lack of interest in books, but the inability to use them efficiently. One can only conclude that either the teaching of reading is not so effective as we like to think it is, or else we entertain the wrong expectations of students if we expect them to be book lovers.

The problem is well illustrated by the case of the student who recently consulted the author about his lack of reading ability. After a period in industry the student had entered university to read for a degree in engineering, but he was deeply worried because he was not able to read as quickly and efficiently as he thought he should do. Discussion of the problem revealed a complete lack of knowledge about how to tackle not only advanced reading, but also essential related study skills such as note-making and cross referencing information. This is a more common failing than we realise, but need not be such an acute problem if it was tackled systematically in the schools.

The suggestions outlined in the previous chapter were designed to provide a structured framework within which a start could be made towards a solution of the problem, but if it is to be tackled effectively the systematic development of reading skills must be continued in the secondary school. Thus what is required is a reading programme for the secondary school which will extend the skills developed at the middle school level. Obviously if the programmes are truly developmental, some of the ideas suggested for the middle school programme would be applicable also to the early stages of secondary education.

## THE SPECIALIST ROLE IN THE SECONDARY SCHOOL

Many large secondary schools have a reading specialist on the staff who has the expertise to advise his colleagues about reading skills. Usually, however, such teachers are in charge of remedial education and this in itself is a full-time job. It is unlikely, in any case, that the teacher of, say, mathematics or science at sixth form or high school level would think of turning to the remedial teacher for advice about reading, even though sixth-form students would probably have much to gain from a mastery of advanced reading skills. The task calls for a reading specialist whose sphere of influence is wider than that of the remedial specialist and whose expertise is of a rather different nature.

Since reading is a specialised language skill it would seem obvious that a qualification in language would be a prerequisite for the holder of such a post. The school librarian would seem to be one possibility. By virtue of his task he should have some knowledge of advanced study skills, for instance the use of the library as a resource for learning. Usually the librarian also has the necessary language qualifications and by the very nature of the job he also has the necessary contacts with all the various departments of a school to enable him to both advise and to co-ordinate activities. There seems to be no good reason why the librarian in a large school should not be appointed to the post full time with the status and role of the tutor-librarian as, for example, in a college of education.

Apart from advising and co-ordinating the tutor-librarian would also be expected to have a specific teaching role. Amongst other things he might organise short courses on study skills which would include such aspects of study as the effective use of a library. This would be of value to all students who intend taking advanced academic examinations, for instance those taken preparatory to entering university or other institute of higher education, and direct and specific teaching would be more effective than if the development of study skills were left to chance. If reading and study skills are to be fully and systematically developed it would be advisable that there be the maximum liaison with reading specialists in the feeder schools for two important reasons. Firstly, such co-operation would help to ensure continuity of progression for the children; and secondly, the secondary school specialist would know what knowledge he might reasonably expect the children to have when they transfer to the secondary school.

If a systematic programme of reading and study skills were developed it would be more likely to ensure that students are equipped to study at an advanced level when they leave school, and it would, therefore, probably prove both economical and beneficial for those students who go on to any form of higher education.

One would see the tutor-librarian as a reading specialist operating at two levels :

(a) In direct teaching he would be responsible for giving specific instruction in such study skills as the use of library facilities and the use of advanced reference material. He might also be responsible for advising on the techniques of note-making and the preparation of assignments.

All these aspects should be developed into a reading programme which would refer to a whole range of materials and be constructed in such a way as to provide for the systematic development of reading skills. It could be closely structured if it is believed that the learning is best achieved when the material to be learned is broken down into small steps to ensure success, which may well be necessary in the case of slower learners. On the other hand, the programme might be quite loosely structured and flexible, providing general guidance for students who are quick learners. Whichever of these approaches is adopted, it would be advisable to spell out certain objectives which the students should achieve by the end of the programme.

(b) The advisory role is an important one made necessary because the job specification of the subject specialist tends to limit his objectives. Further limitations are placed upon him by examination requirements. All too often he has to plan the students' reading himself and this is usually restricted to the basic text books. Thus the students come to rely on him for guidance and are not encouraged to develop and use their own learning skills and their own methods and patterns of study. The reading specialist's role here would be to advise colleagues on how to develop these skills within the context of a discipline. The subject specialist could then use this knowledge in order to guide students' learning within his own special field of study. He might, for instance, spend some time discussing with students sources of material and the setting up of objectives for a unit of study. This should help the students to become more self-reliant and independent as learners.

FUNCTIONAL READING IN THE SECONDARY SCHOOL

The objectives suggested in this chapter are intended to extend the students' skill in functional reading to a more advanced level commensurate with the work which they will normally undertake in the secondary school. As in the case of the middle school, specialist subject teachers should be aware of these objectives in setting assignments for students.

At the end of their secondary school course the students should have developed the following skills thoroughly:

(i) The use of library card index files.
(ii) The use of other bibliographic aids.
(iii) The use of advanced reference material, for instance the use of specialist encyclopedias and works of reference.

If these skills have been fully developed the students should know how to go about finding information systematically and easily. They should also have developed the use of methodical reading when searching for information. Roberts,[1] in outlining possible approaches to the development of some of these information retrieval skills, suggests that they may be applicable to advanced reading in the later stages of the primary school, but two in particular, viz. skimming and SQ3R, seem to be more suited to secondary school work.

Mastery of skimming as a skilled technique for efficient and rapid reading depends upon a knowledge of, and ability to use, the constraints of language. It is a skill which is badly used when it is used at all, and Roberts suggests that it can be systematically developed in the classroom situation so that it may be adopted by students as an effective learning skill (see Roberts, page 70).

SQ3R (survey, question, read, recall, review)[2] is an advanced technique recommended to students by the Open University in their study guide. It is a technique which would have to be practised regularly, preferably under the direct guidance of the teacher, until it is used habitually. There are five stages in adopting this method of studying:

(i) Survey the material in total to get a general view of what has to be studied in detail. (In the case of a book this would include referring to the table of contents, chapter headings, summaries, etc.).
(ii) Devise questions based upon the survey which one would expect to be able to answer after studying the text.
(iii) Read the material through.
(iv) After each section recall the salient points and make notes of what has been read.
(v) Review the reading and test the accuracy of note-making by going over the four previous steps again.

Mastery of such techniques as those outlined above would be of considerable value to all students undertaking any form of advanced academic work.

If reading skills are to be truly effective they should be developed, as has already been implied, within the context of a programme of study skills. Functional reading skills are specialised study skills which for successful application should be supported by skill in note-making and recording. Thus an important element of any reading programme at this level should be guidance for students on the following points:

(i) How to select the material required in order to tackle a given problem successfully.
(ii) How to organise the information obtained from reference sources into meaningful units for future reference. (This becomes of special importance when students are using a variety of sources to obtain information.)
(iii) In order to help the students to organise their material they also need some guidance on writing-up notes. Most of them require specific instruction in how to summarise what they read and how to develop outlines for notes or assignments. These skills tend to be taken for granted, but the author knows from experience that many students have some difficulty in taking useful and relevant notes; they do require help and guidance:

A programme such as this can be geared to academic learning at several levels. It can be made quite simple if the academic content is not very high, or it can be made an advanced course of study skills for higher levels of learning.

READING, LANGUAGE AND THE CURRICULUM

The suggestions made so far in this chapter would seem to be of greater relevance and application to the more academic secondary school student. How far they can be applied to those students who are less academically inclined will depend on several factors, not least the curriculum being followed by these students. A reading programme developed within a language course in which the emphasis is on the active use of language would probably be more relevant to both the present and future needs of the non-academic student.

A course of this nature could be based upon communication as a two-way process; the communication between the self and others, and the understanding and interpretation of modes of communication between others and the self. Many aspects of present-day society would seem to indicate the need for courses of this nature at secondary school level.

An inter-disciplinary pragmatic approach to the curriculum would probably meet the needs of the non-academic, secondary school student better than the more traditional intra-disciplinary approach. Thus within the context of a study of language, the reading skills necessary to cope with everyday problems might be more successfully developed since in this situation the students are more likely to see their relevance. Language work might usefully include the following suggestions amongst others:

(i) All the students will at some time or another have to complete certain forms, even if it is only an application for a driving licence or the electoral roll return. Forms of any kind can be pretty daunting and few, if any, of us really enjoy filling them in. But familiarity with forms, knowing what is required and how to follow instructions (which are sometimes far from clear) can help to dispel the anxiety attached to form filling, especially when the practice is undertaken with nothing at stake so that mistakes don't greatly matter. Some legal forms, such as hire-purchase agreements, require very careful reading and make considerable demands on comprehension skills. Such forms could be studied by groups of children, each group taking one part of the contract or one set of instructions and sifting out the essential and most important information.

(ii) Reading skills of a different kind can be developed by comparing the treatment of news items in a number of newspapers. Every secondary school should take a wide selection of daily papers such that the political views represented range across the spectrum. By studying the treatment of a particular news item in each of the papers, noting what each one includes in its report and what is left out, students will be able to get a fuller and more balanced picture of the item under consideration. They will also become aware that any news report is an edited version of a particular event which usually represents one person's point of view.

Group study of newspaper advertising and such documents as travel brochures can also help to develop skilled critical reading. In this case, the students should examine carefully just what they are told, abstracting from the descriptions of goods, hotels, items, etc. the essential information. They should then ask themselves what further information is necessary if they are to have the full picture, since this is usually of vital importance. An example of the kind of deception which is practised is the advertisement for a digital watch which was carried by many national daily papers. As watches usually have a metal case it is natural to assume that all watches are so made. In this instance the case was made of plastic, but this information was not contained in the advertisement. Much gullibility on the part of the public could be prevented if reading skills were fully developed in schools.

(iii) A third element of a language and reading programme for the less academically inclined secondary school student should include a study of, and practice in, personal communication both in a face-to-face situation and over spatial distance, including communication by letter, telephone and telegram. We tend to take such communication for granted. The emphasis is usually placed on the actual process of sending a message, for instance instruction in how to lay out a letter or address an envelope; the possible effect on the person receiving the message is all too often forgotten. The telephone is, to some extent, an intrusion on one's privacy which demands an immediate response. The letter, on the other hand, gives an initial warning about the contents on the envelope; either the person receiving it can open it straight away or it can be left until later if this is desired. The response can be premeditated to a greater extent than can the response to a telephone message. These aspects of communication are of importance in everyday life and should not be overlooked in the classroom.

One might also usefully include in this element of language study the use of language in various social situations, for example the simulated interview, in which the behaviour of both the interviewer and the interviewee is discussed. When one starts to think along these lines a wide range of possibilities is opened up to the perceptive and understanding teacher.

The study of language should reflect the linguistic process, that is it should be alive and active not dead and passive. The approach suggested here is intended to create in secondary school students an awareness of the importance of language, of its value as a means of communication and of expression.

RECREATIONAL READING IN THE SECONDARY SCHOOL

It is a pity that recreational reading is not taken more seriously at secondary school level. If literature is considered at all it is more often than not done so because of the necessity of studying for examinations. No matter how heavy the curriculum there should still be time for reading for pleasure, time for browsing in the library and time for discussing books. Many of the ideas suggested in the previous chapter would not be out of place in the secondary school. New books by promising or favourite authors should be bought regularly for the library and advertised by means of dust-jacket displays and book reviews. Reading specialised fiction could also supplement the students' basic text-book reading in many of the disciplines; this often adds interest to the studies and encourages the student to adopt a fresh perspective on the work under consideration.

The less academic student creates special problems. He is unlikely to lean naturally towards books as a source of recreation and enjoyment and any approach which is designed to interest him will require careful thought in the planning. The suggestions made with regard to children in the middle school would seem to be especially applicable in this case, and one would strongly recommend the use of television programmes and films as a stimulus to reading. Novels, or parts of novels, related to topics being studied in school could be read either by the whole class or by groups of students and discussed critically in the light of other reading of a more factual nature.

Contemporary novels which deal with social problems are also worth exploring and provided they are chosen with care they can be a useful springboard for social education.

## SUMMARY

If reading skills are to be fully developed as effective study skills then it is essential that they are systematically taught and used in the secondary school as well as at earlier stages of education. The teaching should be in the hands of a specialist with (a) a sound knowledge of advanced reading and study skills, and (b) contact with specialist teachers throughout the school.

For many of the students at secondary level the development of reading skills cannot easily be divorced from the wider study of language behaviour and language development. The approach to studying language at this level could be more active and imaginative than it tends to be in many schools. The present emphasis on correct use of language could be balanced by a study of the influence of language on others. Students should be made aware of its importance both as a medium of communication and as a means of expression, and the best way of developing this awareness is by using language in a variety of contexts. We learn more about language by using it as well as observing it in use than we do by observation alone.

## NOTES

1  G. R. Roberts, *Reading in Primary Schools* (London, Routledge, 1969), pp. 68–71.
2  G. H. McLaughlan and C. R. Coles, 'Efficient Reading 1 and 2', in *New Education*, Work Papers 10 and 11 (1966).

*Chapter 6*

# The Problem of Reading Failure

The publication in 1972 of a government-sponsored survey of reading standards attracted wide attention.[1] Because the researchers found no significant increase in standards since the results of a similar survey were published in 1964 the report gave rise to some concern amongst educationalists and led to the setting up of a commission of inquiry into the teaching of reading at all levels.

Such surveys are useful indicators of trends, but they are of limited value as direct aids to the teacher in the classroom.

The purpose of this chapter is to examine briefly some of the evidence which seems to indicate that reading failure is a complex problem which admits of no easy solution. But the teacher in the classroom can take steps to alleviate the problem in individual cases, as will be discussed in the next chapter.

## THE EXTENT OF READING FAILURE

Whilst the survey of Start and Wells is open to criticism on several grounds, one cannot lightly dismiss their report. Above all, the strong implication that all is not well with the way in which reading is at present taught in many schools cannot be ignored and indeed gives rise to considerable cause for concern. We should not be too surprised at this conclusion. Morris[2] in her survey of reading in Kent schools found that there was a tendency for children who were classed as slow readers at 7 years of age to remain poor readers throughout their school careers. (Crawford's[3] research indicates that some of these slow readers at 7 are not necessarily unintelligent in the generally accepted sense of the term.) Other evidence as to the extent of the problem has come from the large-scale surveys carried out by the National Child Development Survey under the direction of Dr L. Kellmer Pringle.[4]

Reading failure may be the result of some physiological or neurological defect in the individual child, but recent studies, including those mentioned earlier, indicate that in many cases failure is due to causes rooted in the socio-cultural milieu of a considerable number of children. The attitudes, values and expectations of both the home and the school are thought to be among the important contributory causes. Wiseman[5] has shown that parental attitudes are probably a critical factor in measuring academic success. Especially influential is the attitude of the home to books and reading; 'literacy, as evinced by measures of reading and library membership, proves to be a highly significant measure in all analyses of individual pupils'.[6]

All the evidence would seem to point to a two-fold problem. On the one hand there are those individual children whose reading problems are the result of some physical or neurological defect. Such children usually require highly specialised individual teaching. There is also a much bigger problem, less clearly defined but more widespread where the root cause of reading difficulty lies in the total environment of quite large numbers of children; and this is predominantly confined to specific urban areas. These are the children who would benefit most from the systematic teaching of reading skills.

## THE CLASSIFICATION OF READING PROBLEMS

The solution of reading problems is not made any easier by lack of clear definition and a failure to devise a definitive aetiology within which to classify them with some degree of precision. The terms 'backwardness in reading' and 'reading failure' are in themselves so wide as to be of limited value. (One reason why the term 'reading problems' is preferable is that it implies a multiplicity of factors which may be analysed in trying to diagnose the cause of failure of any individual child.)

The earliest studies of reading problems both in this country and in the United States of America placed considerable emphasis on physical and intellectual factors found within the child, although some authorities, such as Burt,[7] indicated that causal factors may be found in the environment.

Schonell[8] illustrates the gradual development of a more systematic classification of causal factors in reading failure. He identified five factors in reading ability which act inter-dependently to produce skilled, fluent reading, but which may, conversely, also be causes of reading failure. They are:

(i) General maturity.
(ii) Level of general intelligence.
(iii) Abilities of visual and auditory recognition and discrimination of word patterns.

(iv) Environmental factors in reading ability.
(v) Emotional attitudes of interest, individual application and confidence.

These can be classified under three broad headings as factors associated with the child, the home and the school. Of these three areas the child has probably been the most fully researched, whilst the school is the least explored area and the one which may be most rewarding in further research. The model suggested by Ravenette in his book, *Dimensions of Reading Difficulties*[9] is refreshing for its different approach to this problem of classification of reading problems. He questions whether we have adopted the right approach in the past and suggests that it might be more profitable to consider dimensions within which observations can be made about reading failure:

'Every profession is concerned with sets of issues or problems which can be defined in relation to dimensions which are relevant to that profession, for instance for doctors the dimension of health or illness is vitally important. The dimensions provide the frame of reference within which problems are understood, and at their simplest represent points of view. The problems of reading and reading difficulties can be seen from a number of different points of view, or dimensions. Each dimension can be used to enlighten the problem. ... No single dimension is necessarily the best, but any one dimension may be more useful in a given instance.'[10]

Thinking in terms of dimensions along the lines suggested by Ravenette rather than the more traditional approach of looking for causes throws responsibility onto the problem-solvers rather than on the source of the problem, that is in the case of reading, on the teacher rather than on the child. Dimensions also open up areas for exploration, whilst causes all too often become ends in themselves. A dimensional approach affords greater freedom of thought and flexibility of action than does an approach to problems in which the emphasis is on causation.

Ravenette uses the traditional classification of areas within which to define dimensions, that is the child, the home and the school, but to these he adds an extra category of personal dimensions, for example the relationship between child and teacher, a factor not always given sufficient weight in studies of reading failure. In thinking about intersecting dimensions, we may be more likely to ask the right questions about an individual child's failure to master reading.

READING FAILURE IN ADOLESCENCE

The teacher who has to deal with reading failure in the middle or secondary school will almost certainly have to contend with and overcome motivational failure before the reading problems *per se* can be tackled. The developing adolescent has to deal increasingly with abstract concepts and ideas, not least in his reading, and if the child has found school learning to be a struggle he is likely to find it difficult to come to terms with the situation. Thus this is a very real danger period in the school careers of many children, since it is at this time that they are most likely to develop an indifferent or super-cilious attitude, not only towards reading but also towards formal school learning in all its aspects.

It is a multi-faceted problem with strong societal influences at work at both the macro and micro levels. Some of the wider issues were discussed briefly in an earlier chapter when the influence of television on reading attitudes and habits was considered. Here we are looking at rather narrower cultural and environmental correlates of the prob-lem as they affect one section of society in particular. Although the discussion is centred upon reading problems, it has relevance to all such aspects of education as are commonly regarded as book learning.

Since the early work of Burt,[11] whose extensive surveys have been a seminal influence on all later research in Britain, reading failure has come to be strongly associated with what is now called social underprivilege. In Burt's work, which was largely undertaken in pre-war London, this was seen almost entirely in material terms, but today we are more concerned with such factors as attitudes with-in the family, interaction between home and school and, as is obvious from this book amongst many others, the role of language. Our main concern is to examine the possible effects which these factors might have on the development of literacy.

While few can deny the importance of home background there has been a change of emphasis from the home to the school as a possible contributory cause of reading failure, and the learning environment of the school may yet turn out to be a key factor in the problem. Teaching skill is of obvious importance, but evidence from research indicates that methods of teaching, attitudes and relationships and what Brandis and Henderson call 'cultural discontinuity'[12] (essen-

tially whether school makes sense to the learner) are all possible con-
comitants of reading failure.

There appears to be little doubt that reading failure is more
frequently found among children from the lower socio-economic
classes of society (classes IV and V on the Registrar General's classification*) than it is among those from occupational classes I and II.
(See, for instance, Kellmer Pringle's study of 11,000 7-year-old children.)[13] Although there is some doubt as to whether low social class
is a causal or predisposing factor in reading attainment,[14] it does seem
clear that 'homes in different socio-economic classes show marked
cultural differences which are likely to affect the children's linguistic
ability, and this in turn is related to reading achievement'.[15] The
evidence of Wiseman reported earlier in this chapter is supported by
that of Morris[16] who found a positive relationship between reading
ability and the number of adult books and newspapers in the home
and parental membership of public libraries. The main effect of these
environmental factors would seem to be upon the cognitive abilities
of the children and especially upon their motivation to learn. There
is no doubt about the existence of a relationship between parental
attitude to achievement and the academic success of the child, and
encouragement in this respect is more likely to be a feature of homes
in the higher rather than in the lower social classes. This applies
from the earliest stages of formal education. It would seem that, with
regard to reading in particular, children from a lower socio-economic
environment are not only less well prepared to tackle the difficult
early stages of reading, but that they get less support at home even
if they do successfully master the basic skills. Parents who are
anxious for their children to be academically successful are more
likely to ensure that there is a good supply of reading matter in the
home and that their children use the library services regularly when
they are sufficiently proficient at reading. Children from lower
working-class homes are less likely to receive such help, although it
is the author's opinion, and this is backed by some experience, that
many of these parents would help their children more if they were
made fully aware of the issues involved and told how they could best
be of assistance to them. Where a child seldom or never sees books at

* Social class is very difficult to define but in Britain the following classification, based upon the 1951 population census, is generally accepted:

    Class 1   Uppper professional and higher managerial workers.
    Class 2   Lower professional, managerial and upper clerical workers.
    Class 3   Skilled manual workers.
    Class 4   Semi-skilled workers.
    Class 5   Unskilled workers.

home he is unlikely to see the necessity for learning to read, and he is consequently unlikely to be appreciative of the long-term value of literacy.

We can see, therefore, that interest and desire to achieve do play an important part in motivating children to read, and those who find it difficult will probably need special stimulation in school. How is the teacher to do this? While one can suggest no single answer it might help to look at three areas over which individual teachers have some measure of control.

The first of these, the reading environment, has already been mentioned in a previous chapter, but it is of sufficient importance as to warrant special emphasis; probably because this aspect of reading is so obvious it is often overlooked and neglected. Readers who remember public libraries of the pre-war era will perhaps have a clearer understanding of the problem. The only thing which encouraged the author to use this service with its predominantly Victorian drabness and forbidding silence was the fact that here was a very cheap source of both enjoyment and knowledge. Present-day libraries with their bright displays and books in protected dust covers present a much more stimulating environment. Unfortunately, the reading environment of many schools resembles the pre-war library rather than the contemporary one. Education is largely about books and they should always be prominently and attractively displayed. Even if this is difficult to achieve in the school, the individual teacher can do much in his own classroom with book displays on current projects or topics of interest. In the case of slow readers it is essential that the books are attractively produced with clear and legible print and colourful illustrations. The success of such a display in achieving its objective can be assessed by the amount and kind of use to which the books are subjected.

Another area over which the individual teacher has some degree of control is that of method of approach. One would hesitate to use the usual classification of formal and informal methods, a more satisfactory classification is perhaps the one which is implicit throughout this book, namely an active or passive approach to language and reading. This may imply an individual or small group rather than a class learning situation, although obviously the latter might be more suitable in story-telling or poetry reading. Certainly, as has been stated previously, use should be made of the children's own language as a basis for a variety of reading experiences, especially in topic work and in much of the written work. With slow-learning children, an integrated approach to language study is probably more likely to be effective than one which sees the various facets of language as separate elements in the curriculum. Children are more likely to experiment with spoken language than they are with written language and this can lead to an interest in the use of language which might stimulate them to develop their reading.* The selected reading experiences provided for slow readers should be so structured that the learner is able to make successful progress in his reading development and also be aware of an increasing mastery of the reading process. This will require the careful planning of reading programmes designed to meet individual needs, and would probably be more easily accomplished within a framework which outlines the reading skills necessary for the development of literacy. An approach to reading along these lines would be more likely to ensure consistent development than one which leaves progression to chance.

Last, but not least in importance, the teacher can have regard to his relationships with the children and attitudes towards them. These can be a crucial factor in dealing with children, particularly if they lack a satisfactory self-image which is all too often the case with slow-learning children. The work of Rosenthal and Jacobson in the United States of America[17] indicates that the self-fulfilling prophecy may well be a valid concept if applied to academic achievement. Teachers who expect a low standard of work from children are unlikely to get work of a high standard from them. Rosenthal and Jacobson in one of their experiments told a group of teachers that certain chil-

---

*I am aware that in frequent textual references to the differences between speech and writing I can be accused of simplifying a highly complex relationship. Those who take this view may well disagree that children are more likely to experiment with spoken language than they are with the written word. Many teachers are familiar with linguistic experimentation in the field of imaginative/creative writing, but there seems to be a dearth of serious investigation of the quality of imaginative verbal responses in the classroom.

I would support my argument by reference to the following:
(a) Some current research in which I am studying the quality of children's written response in imaginative writing. As the research has progressed I have become increasingly convinced of the value and importance of verbal language experiences as a sound basis for imaginative written work.
(b) The firm belief that a verbal response is not subject to such strong constraints as a written response. Children tend to think twice before they write a word, phrase or sentence (as indeed I have had to do in preparing this manuscript); they are much more spontaneous in verbal responses. In my research children have often given me good, imaginative verbal responses but they have not always used them in their subsequent written work.

dren, who had been selected at random by the experimenters, could be expected to show an intellectual spurt within the academic year. On re-testing at the end of the year the children selected for mention were found to have fulfilled the prophecy. While insufficient research has been undertaken to establish this as a behavioural norm, practising teachers are well aware that the principle applies to social aspects of behaviour, for example the boy who is repeatedly told that he is naughty comes to accept the role of a naughty boy and naughtiness as his norm of behaviour. If this applies to social behaviour, there seems to be no good reason why academic behaviour should not be similarly affected. This is, of course, not to argue that we should have unrealistic expectations of children with learning difficulties, but that we should try to make an objective assessment of their present capabilities so that future progress may be more securely based.

It is important that children who are apathetic or resentful at school should achieve some measure of success in their learning, and that this should be acknowledged by words of encouragement and praise from the teacher. Teaching skill is necessary to make the learning situations stimulating, interesting and relevant, but over and above this children who find school difficult need encouragement, success and recognition. In order to establish optimum working conditions in this difficult learning situation, the teacher should try to establish firm and stable but understanding relationships with the children. The teacher needs to be friendly and sympathetic, but not to such an extent that the children take control of the classroom situation. The author's experience is that they prefer strong leadership from the teacher and an orderly approach to their work. The tasks which they are set should be clearly defined so that the children are under no misapprehension as to what they are expected to do. So often this is the pattern of their lives outside school, especially where they only have a narrow choice of activities, that they either find some difficulty in coming to terms with a situation which is too open-ended or alternatively they quickly learn to exploit it. The secret of teaching success, in so far as there is one, would seem to lie in the skill of the teacher in setting up interesting learning situations which enable the children to make progress at their own individual rate and in responding positively to successful learning outcomes.

While this may seem to be quite straightforward with regard to learning in the classroom, it does imply other important wider issues. What we are really examining are ways of minimising the conflict which is believed to exist between the culture of children from lower working-class homes and that of the school. The problem is clearly stated by Carroll:

'His [the child's] teachers must ponder the extent to which they can simply build upon his previously acquired capabilities and the extent to which they can alter a system of habits which are not only highly practised, but which also probably serve a supportive role in the child's adjustment to his non-school environment.'[18]

These problems present a challenge to our professional skills as teachers and to avoid them is to shirk our duty to many children. There is no easy solution to them; one can only suggest certain possible lines of approach which individual teachers might find applicable in given situations.

SUMMARY

The last twenty-five years have seen a great increase in both psychological and sociological research into reading problems. There is greater accuracy in defining reading failure, but because of the vast output of research papers an individual teacher would probably find it difficult to know what was and what was not relevant to a particular problem. Since much of this work is of interest to many teachers and is often of practical application in the classroom there would seem to be a need for the classification of the research into clearly defined areas of the reading process.

There has been a change of emphasis in much recent research from the child to the environment in the search for causal factors of failure. Some surveys indicate that this may be a prime agent. Whilst the home has still the strongest influence upon a child's attitudes, values and expectations, it is now realised that the school, and particularly the individual teacher, can be of considerable importance in influencing attitudes towards books and learning. Studies of environmental factors in reading failure have also led to a reconsideration of motivational failure, shown by many researchers to be closely associated with the socio-cultural background of the learner. Thus the teacher faced with reading problems at the middle or secondary school level is often faced with the key problem of overcoming failure in motivation before he can concentrate on specific reading problems.

NOTES

1   K. B. Start and B. K. Wells, *The Trend of Reading Standards* (Slough, NFER, 1972).

2   J. M. Morris, *Standards and Progress in Reading* (Slough, NFER, 1966).

3   A. Crawford, Unpublished manuscript of research undertaken into the incidence of reading failure at junior school level in Liverpool (Liverpool, 1966).

4   R. Davie, N. Butler and H. Goldstein, *From Birth to Seven* (London, Longmans, 1972).

5   HMSO, *Children and the Primary Schools: The Plowden Report* (London, HMSO, 1967), Vol. 2.

6   Ibid, p. 382.

7   C. Burt, *The Backward Child* (London, University of London Press, 1937).

8   F. J. Schonell, *The Psychology and Teaching of Reading* (Edinburgh, Oliver & Boyd, 1945).

9   A. T. Ravenette, *Dimensions of Reading Difficulties* (Oxford, Pergamon Press, 1968).

10  Ibid., p. 6.

11  Burt, op. cit.

12  W. Brandis and D. Henderson, *Social Class, Language and Communication* (London, Routledge, 1970)

13  M. L. Kellmer Pringle, N. R. Butler and R. Davie, *11,000 Seven-Year-Olds* (London, Longmans, 1966).

14  K. Lovell and M. E. Woolsey, 'Reading Disability, Non-Verbal Reasoning and Social Class', in *Educational Research*, Vol. 6 (1964), p. 226.

15  M. D. Vernon, 'The Effect of Motivational and Emotional Factors on Learning to Read', in J. F. Reid (ed.), *Reading: Problems and Practices* (London, Ward Lock Educational for the Open University, 1973), p. 50. (This article contains a very clear account of the psychological aspects of the problem.)

16  Morris, op. cit.

17  R. Rosenthal and L. F. Jacobson, *Pygmalion in the Classroom* (New York, Holt, Rinehart & Winston, 1968).

18  J. B. Carroll, 'Language Development in Children', in S. Saporta (ed.), *Psycho-linguistics* (New York, Holt, Rinehart & Winston, 1961), p. 342.

# Chapter 7

# The Diagnosis and Treatment of Reading Problems

Children whose reading is severely retarded are usually quickly diagnosed and referred for remedial treatment because their disability affects their academic work to such an extent that the class teacher or subject teachers find they constitute a serious problem. Less fortunate are those children, and they may be more numerous than we care to admit, who have just mastered the basic mechanics of reading with a struggle. Very often the progress of these children towards becoming skilled, fluent readers tends to slow down or even stop altogether once they have passed the first school stage of their education. They are seldom given the help they really need, largely because we see reading as a total process, a total skill which is acquired in the earliest stages of education or not at all.

If, however, we regard reading as a developmental process depending for success upon the mastery of sub-skills or second-order skills at a sequence of levels, then the problem becomes more manageable. Many children between the ages of 8 and 12 fail to develop into skilled readers because they are not taught how to use reading skills within a sequential developmental framework. Once the basic skills appear to have been mastered further reading development is largely left to chance, mainly because of the widely held belief that most children are skilled readers at 7 years of age. (This despite the fact that much research, including the author's own, indicates that such is not the case.)

A skill approach to reading provides the teacher with a structured framework within which more accurate diagnosis of individual differences is made possible. The situation is analogous to the difference between the layman's view of the petrol engine and that of the mechanic; the complex totality defeats most laymen, but the mechanic, faced with engine failure, is able to diagnose it more easily because he is able to see the engine as the sum of several constituent parts and thus he can isolate the source of failure. Improved diagnosis should in turn make it easier for the teacher to prescribe individual reading programmes to help slower readers overcome their difficulties. But the success of this approach to reading difficulties depends, in the last analysis, upon skilled teaching of a high order. For instance, it will require much more of a teacher than simply hearing a child read aloud and helping him with words and phrases which cause difficulty. Such sessions when undertaken with slow readers are perhaps better regarded as counselling or tutorial sessions in which the mistakes made by the reader are carefully analysed as part of a diagnostic programme. They should have clearly defined aims and objectives which would give reading lessons much more point and purpose than is commonly the case.

## SCREENING, DIAGNOSIS AND TREATMENT

Teachers tend to place too much reliance on the use of standardised reading tests in assessing reading ability and diagnosing difficulties. In some respects this is understandable since the tests tend to be given a seal of approval by experts in the field and to be used extensively in research. It is possible that the importance attached to testing in the interests of producing sound research programmes may have a deleterious effect upon their general usefulness. This is not to imply that the use of tests be condemned out of hand, but rather to question their purpose and suggest that there should be some re-thinking about their value as diagnostic tools. It is probable that in dealing with individual children skilled and accurate observation can often provide the teacher with more information about individual children than a whole battery of tests.

Diagnosis should be at two levels. Standardised tests would be used in the initial screening in order to obtain information about the general level of reading ability and to select those children who appear to be at risk of failing as well as those who are obviously having serious difficulties. Children who fall into the latter category should be referred for remedial reading if they are not already undergoing treatment. The problems of those who appear to be at risk should be analysed further using the teacher's own observations and diagnostic techniques in order to define areas of failure and prescribe treatment.

All children should be tested to assess their reading ability when they transfer to another school, especially on transfer to the middle or secondary school. Since large numbers of children would be involved in a screening programme of this nature, one of the many group tests of reading ability, of the type published by the National

Foundation for Educational Research (NFER) for instance, might best serve this purpose. The results would give some indication of the general standard of reading of an intake of children and would isolate those who may require special teaching. Children with reading ages of more than two years below their chronological ages will probably require special treatment. The ones we should be most concerned about are those whose reading age is about one year to eighteen months below their chronological age. These are the children who will really have to struggle with the more advanced academic work in the secondary school and the ones for whom least help seems to be available.

At this level of reading ability poorly developed phonic skills and lack of skill in attacking new words have been identified as two important areas of weakness. In order to help these children overcome their difficulties the teacher might organise a remedial programme which would include sessions when they read aloud to him. Passages to be used in these sessions should be carefully selected to provide the teacher with information about specific difficulties. Tape-recorded reading sessions are a useful and valuable additional aid made easier by the introduction of the cassette tape-recorder. By using recordings the teacher can keep a permanent record of each child's progress if he so wishes, but more importantly he can analyse mistakes more accurately when he can stop the tape and make notes. If the passages used for reading aloud are printed on a card the teacher can use the tape and the accompanying card like a music score with abbreviated notes made on the text and the final analysis of the session written up in note form for future reference and planning.

A reading programme for slower readers requiring practice in word attack skills might also include a variety of word games such as *Scrabble* and *Lexicon* and problems such as simple crossword puzzles. The teacher's pamphlet to the BBC series 'Look and Read' contains many good ideas which can be adapted by the enterprising teacher.

RECORD KEEPING (See Appendix 2)

Full and accurate record keeping is necessary in cases where individual reading programmes have been devised for the learner. Lack of accurate records can create difficulties when a child changes school, or even when he changes classes. Continuity of progress is as necessary to reading development if it is to be progressive as it is to other skill subjects. The cumulative record card is usually of limited value in this respect since there is seldom sufficient room for detailed records to be kept in any individual subject. (There is perhaps a case to be made out for keeping full records of progress in reading and mathematics for all children.) A systematic and comprehensive record of reading progress should contain information classified along the following lines:

## 1  Background information

*Objective data.* This is the normal data which one would expect to find on any record and would include such details as name, date of birth, position in family, and the results of any standardised tests which have been administered. When recording test scores it is important that the name of the test, the date of testing, and the child's age in years and completed months be recorded.

*Health data.* This is very important, especially information about the child's vision and hearing. The most reliable source of this information, apart from that which may be supplied by parents, is the child's medical record and this is not always easily available.

*School attendance and attainment.* Information about these aspects of the child's background is both useful and important if the teacher is to build up a full profile of him. The cumulative record card and the attendance register will provide relevant information which can be classified under this heading. Special attention should be given to attitudes towards school generally, but also towards particular subjects or areas of the curriculum in this section.

*Interests.* This can be a most useful section if it is kept fully documented. It could be especially valuable in providing possible avenues of approach when dealing with those children who are apathetic or hostile to school learning. Much of the information recorded under this heading can be obtained by careful observation of behaviour, but dialogue between teacher and pupil can also be very useful. More specific details about reading habits at home, television viewing and favourite sports can be obtained by means of direct oral questioning in discussion with the child. If this approach is used, the teacher might be advised to draw up a loosely structured questionnaire, always remembering that a too formal approach may well be counter productive with the children whom we are considering here.

## 2 Reading Ability

*The basic skills.* This is the group of skills which must be mastered successfully in the early stages of learning if skilled reading is going to develop satisfactorily, and covers all those skills associated with pre-reading and the early stages of reading. It is generally accepted that they should be mastered during the earliest stages of schooling, that is between the ages of 5 and 7 years, but many children, possibly a majority, need longer than two years to master them. It is arguable that the arbitrary imposition of a two-year course on the basics of reading is responsible for a good deal of later failure.

Children who are still failing at this level at the middle or more especially at the secondary school stage may well require specialised remedial treatment.

*Comprehension skills.* It is in the progressive mastery of these skills that one is really able to observe reading development. Obviously if the basic skills have been inadequately mastered it is probable that comprehensive skills will be poorly developed. But some children, having mastered the basic skills, never really develop a wide range of comprehension skills because they are not taught as systematically as the basic skills. It is, perhaps, not sufficiently recognised that comprehension skills are developed at several levels. (The one most commonly taught in schools consists of the children answering questions on a short piece of prose or poem which they have read.) But these skills also include the ability to select and understand ideas, the ability to organise one's information into meaningful units, and the ability to find answers to specific questions. On another level, the ability to follow the plot of a story, to be able to relate to the characters in a story or novel are also comprehension skills in which development can be systematically aided by the teacher, as was suggested in Chapter 4.

## 3 Diagnosis, Treatment and Evaluation

*Diagnosis.* This section of a record should obviously include a summary of the main areas of weakness, based upon the teacher's tests and observations. It would also be useful to include some comment on causal factors if this information is known, but this is not always easy to do accurately because reading problems are seldom caused by any one clearly identifiable factor.

*Recommendations for treatment.* These should be set out in detail. It is not enough to carry such information in one's head, as many teachers try to do. Remedial treatment is too important to be put at risk through faulty memory. It is only when a programme is written down that one can see its development and possible lines of progress. Too often this aspect of recording is dealt with in summary fashion to the detriment of the learner.

*Evaluation of progress.* This should be undertaken at regular intervals in order to assess progress. If the prescribed treatment is not proving effective then the teacher must revise the remedial programme. An evaluation programme would probably include the use of standardised tests, but it should also include the teacher's own tests based on the remedial programme. It might also be useful to see whether there has been any change of attitude towards reading in particular and school learning in general.

## SOME BASIC PRINCIPLES OF A REMEDIAL READING PROGRAMME

It is not the purpose of this book to lay down specific remedial programmes to meet the wide range of individual needs for which the teacher will have to cater even if this were possible; but there are certain general principles which are applicable to any remedial programme. A full discussion of this problem is to be found in a paper on basic principles of reading instruction by Bond and Tinker.[1] Essentially, the principles can be classified into two broad categories; those which relate to the child's sense of personal worth, that is aspects which are concerned with the motivation of the failing reader; and those which relate to the teaching programme itself. Some of these principles, for instance that remedial programmes should be tailored to suit the individual child's developmental and learning needs and that they should be systematically structured, are implicit in what has previously been said about remedial reading. Thus, especially at the secondary school level, a reading programme should be so designed not only to motivate the slow reader, but also to enhance his sense of personal worth. It goes without saying that the programme should employ sound teaching procedures, be based upon up-to-date research, and use materials both suited to the child's reading ability and adapted to his age and interest levels.

## SUMMARY

An approach to reading problems based upon skill development would seem to be beneficial to all children for whom reading is a chore not willingly undertaken because of a lack of ability. Given a systematic and structured approach to their problems, these children could become more skilful and efficient readers, but they need teachers who have an awareness of their problems and the requisite knowledge of how they may best be helped. Any teacher should be able to apply to reading basic teaching skills applicable to teaching any other subject in the curriculum, but it would be of value if at least one teacher in each school had sufficient expertise in reading and language problems to be able to advise colleagues about materials to be used and courses of action to be taken. In difficult cases it may be necessary to call upon the services of a specialist teacher from the remedial service to advise upon analysis and subsequent action.

When remedial action is decided upon for individual children full records should be kept containing information about the general background and prescribed treatment. In deciding the form of the records the following points should be kept in mind:

(i) The information recorded should provide the basis upon which future work is developed.

(ii) Record keeping should be regular and systematic. Records should be completed at least once each week, but preferably after each reading session.

(iii) Records should show clearly any development and progress, and the information recorded should be easily understood by anyone consulting the records.

(iv) Care should be taken over the inclusion of any confidential information which may be prejudicial to the child.

(v) Records should be stored for ease of reference when required.

It might also be useful for the children to have records of their own progress. This has not been given much weight in the past, but in the case of children who are not very successful in their school work a record which enables them to see when they are making progress could be beneficial.

If the records show that a child is not making much progress over a period of time then the teacher should re-consider both the content and the methodology of the reading programme. As was stated earlier, these children have all too often suffered from years of failure and frustration, and success is an essential ingredient if they are going to make progress.

NOTES

1 G. L. Bond and M. A. Tinker, 'Basic Principles of Remedial Instruction', in J. F. Reid (ed.), *Reading: Problems and Practices* (London, Ward Lock Educational, 1972), pp. 209–29.

*Chapter 8*

# The Concept of Linguistic Deprivation

### INTRODUCTION

Although the general idea of linguistic deprivation is not new, the concept is of comparatively recent origin and, along with such concepts as compensatory education, has been the subject of much debate.

These concepts have undoubtedly focused attention on problems of which we were previously aware, but which were rather ill-defined. Teachers with wide experience in urban schools have long had to cope with the problems posed by curricula which emphasise book learning for children from homes where books are not part of their environment. The research which has led to the acceptance of deprivation as an educational concept has helped us to define some of these problems with greater clarity and accuracy. The publicity surrounding some of the excellent work being done in inner-city areas, for example Priority in Liverpool, has made many more people aware of these problems. It has also given rise to considerable debate about both curriculum and methods, especially the former, and on a more philosophical level about values and attitudes. A common factor relating to both areas of debate would seem to lie in the experiences of the children. No one would deny that children from urban areas have different experiences from their fellows in suburbia. The teacher is usually more familiar with the latter than the former and tends to use his own perspective as a frame of reference. Such a perspective can only be confusing for children to whom such experiences are foreign. There is no easy answer to this problem. Even if teachers were to live in urban areas, as was tentatively suggested in the Plowden Report, they would be unlikely to share all the experiences of the neighbourhood. But teachers in inner-city schools can make themselves more conversant with the sub-culture of the area through dialogue with both children and parents and through skilful observation. Teaching in urban schools demands teaching skill of a high order, but for it to be fully effective it needs to be allied to a sound understanding of the children's environment.

Phrases such as 'compensatory education' and 'linguistic deprivation' have tended to become emotive terms. Bernstein[1] has criticised the term 'compensatory education' on the grounds that it diverts attention from shortcomings which may well obtain within the school and certainly do obtain within the broad structural framework of the educational system. The word 'compensatory' implies something lacking in the family which must be compensated for within the school. Bernstein's argument is clearly stated in the following passage:

'All that informs the child, that gives meaning and purpose to him outside the school, ceases to be valid and accorded significance and opportunity for enhancement within the school. He has to orient towards a different structure of meaning, whether it is in the form of reading books, in the form of language use and dialect, or in the patterns of social relationships . . . the child is expected, and his parents as well, to drop their social identity, their way of life and its symbolic representation at the school gate. For, by definition, their culture is deprived, the parents inadequate in both the moral and the skill orders they transmit.'[2]

Bernstein suggests, correctly, that we should base much more learning on the children's experience in the family and in the community and, in doing so, give more careful thought to the linguistic environment of the school. This is not, of course, to argue that these experiences should form the parameters of learning, rather that they should form the base from which horizons can be widened for the children. A similar view is echoed by Carroll[3] in discussing language development in children:

'The school can foster the cognitive development of the child best when it is realised that the child brings to his school years a rather large variety of concepts – at least as represented by a large vocabulary – but that the many gaps which still exist in his verbal response system must be filled in as natural a way as possible. This can be done by giving as many pertinent experiences as possible and establishing learning conditions which will allow the child to see relevant distinctions in meaning and differential classification of concepts.'[4]

## DEFINING LINGUISTIC DEPRIVATION

The concept of linguistic deprivation has been strongly attacked both in this country and in the United States of America. It may be argued that since the universals of language are greater than the differentials we should emphasise similarities rather than stress differences in language usage. It is in any case rather patronising to describe as deprived a form of language use which is rooted in an oral tradition and which is often the basis of the folklore of a society. In literate Western societies the language used by the middle class or the professional classes stems from a literary tradition and is therefore strongly influenced by the written word. Evidence to support the view that localised language structures can develop their own aesthetic is seen in the rich language environment of the coloured ghettos in the United States of America[5] from which most of the classic songs of jazz have sprung. In Britain evidence of a rather different nature is to be found in the work of the Opies.[6]

Despite this, one cannot ignore the fact that language is an important element in academic success and therefore in upward social mobility. That the problem may be quite widespread in Western society is evidenced by the School of Barbiana,[7] a group of poor Italian students whose project, fully documented in *Letter to a Teacher*, starts from the premise that school is a war against the poor. These students were neither linguists, psychologists nor sociologists *per se*, but they make some pertinent comments on the implications of language usage:

'. . . we should settle what correct language is. Languages are created by the poor, who then go on renewing them forever. The rich crystallise them in order to put on the spot anybody who speaks in a different way, or in order to make him fail exams.'[8]

Later they state:

'It is language alone that makes men equal. That man is an equal who can express himself and can understand the words of others.'[9]

One of the students who had visited England noted that dialect speech is a barrier to social progress in this country. He comments that we do not fail students in schools, but we divert children to schools of lower quality where 'the poor perfect the art of speaking badly, while the rich keep polishing their language'.[10]

Linguistic deprivation is open to a variety of interpretations, few of which are defined with any degree of clarity. Certainly it cannot be defined in terms of one isolated factor, vocabulary for example, rather it is as complex as language itself. To use the term indiscriminately of large sections of society is to comment on the people themselves as much as on the way in which they use language.

A more satisfactory approach to the problem which also provides a clearer definition is that suggested by Herriot.[11] His arguments are based upon the psychological premise that language is skilled behaviour. If language is a necessary means of (a) communicating, and (b) regulating one's behaviour in society, then it becomes a matter of some importance that language skills should be adequately acquired. Both maturation and experience are necessary elements in the development of linguistic competence and any interference with either of these two elements may well result in an inability to use language skilfully in a wide variety of social situations, or, in other words, in some degree of linguistic deficiency.

Inadequately developed grammatical skills create a special problem when language is used as communication. This is especially relevant to the school situation where the communication of ideas, predominantly by means of the spoken or written word, plays such an important role.

In the adequate development of language skills the mother/child relationship is believed to be of considerable importance. If the mother's own linguistic skills are underdeveloped, the child's language skills would tend to follow the same pattern. The author has himself observed that some mothers, mainly but not always from working-class backgrounds, tend to use language to control behaviour much more often than they use it to comment on, and explain, situations or objects. Used in this way language behaviour tends to be a one-way communication process which does not make for rational discussion but rather encourages the sharp one-word response which is characteristic of many children brought up in this kind of environment. This is the kind of response so often regarded in the school situation as insolent, but given the background in which it is developed one should not be too surprised to hear it.

Defining linguistic deprivation in Herriot's terms seems to make sense. At least it gives some indication as to how the problem might be tackled and implies that it is perhaps safer to refer to individuals or small groups of children as being linguistically deprived rather than to apply the concept without much thought to large sections of the population.

## SOME IMPLICATIONS FOR TEACHERS

The author believes that in the light of the evidence cited above and that of his own experience there should be a radical reappraisal of language teaching at the middle and secondary stages of education.

There should be greater emphasis on the exploration of language, starting early in the middle school and developing greater depth of exploration and analysis in the secondary school. This should not just be confined to the language lessons *per se* but developed across the curriculum so that the children would develop, for instance, a more accurate mathematical or scientific language. Discussion of findings and reporting back, in topic work, for example, would help to keep a balance as between oral and written language; all too often the emphasis is on the latter at the expense of the former, even though most children will use spoken language far more than they will write after leaving school.

This approach is perhaps more difficult to adopt in the secondary school, but the need to develop spoken language is just as great if not greater at this level. The adolescent tends to use language in social situations where talk is one means of reinforcing solidarity with each other, indicating common values, assumptions and experiences. In these situations much may be left un-expressed which would in other circumstances be expressed more formally. These informal experiences do not encourage the use of language in analysis, which is an important element of academic education, and if they are the limit of the learner's oral language experience he will be lacking the linguistic tools necessary to cope with a variety of social and learning situations. Much greater use could be made of simulated interviews, role plays and other experiences calling for the use of spoken language. The young learners should be encouraged to observe and record their own findings and emotions in a wide variety of ways, using, for instance, the tape-recorder as well as the pen. There is no good reason why the language curriculum should not include elements of language study along these lines. They could be developed within a flexible structure with, if necessary, a high standard of academic discipline. Such a programme would have the added advantage of greater relevance to real-life situations which is so often missing from language courses. It would again help to provide an active instead of a passive approach to language studies, and since language is an active process it would be much nearer to reality than the artificiality of parsing a passage of script.

## SUMMARY

The concept of linguistic deprivation has probably been more valuable in posing problems and asking questions than in providing solutions. There is a tendency to use the term too loosely with respect to large groups of people; some evidence would seem to indicate that this is a mistaken approach. Seen in terms of the unsatisfactory development of linguistic skills which are an essential tool of learning, linguistic deprivation may have more relevance and may be more accurately applied to individuals or small groups of children.

Acceptance of the feasibility of the concept would seem to imply a more active oral approach to formal English in the classroom.

NOTES

1  B. Bernstein, *Class, Codes and Control* (London, Routledge, 1971), Vol. 1.
2  Ibid., p. 192.
3  J. B. Carroll, 'Language Development in Children', in S. Saporta (ed.), *Psycho-linguistics* (New York, Holt, Rinehart & Winston, 1961).
4  Ibid., p. 192.
5  See, for instance, H. Ginsberg, *The Myth of the Deprived Child* (New Jersey, Prentice-Hall, 1972).
6  I. Opie and P. Opie, *The Lore and Language of Schoolchildren* (London, Oxford University Press, 1959).
7  School of Barbiana, *Letter to a Teacher* (Harmondsworth, Penguin, 1970).
8  Ibid., p. 24.
9  Ibid., p. 80.
10  Ibid., p. 86.
11  P. Herriot, *Language and Teaching* (London, Methuen, 1971).

# Chapter 9

# A Brief Note on Adult Illiteracy

The purpose of this short chapter is two-fold. In the first place, if this book is read in conjunction with Taylor's companion volume, *Reading and Writing in the First School*,[1] it should present the reader with a total overview of the reading process. Secondly, it is intended to sound a note of warning about some possible consequences for the children if we fail them in respect of literacy.

It is easy to assume that universal education, which has been the norm in Britain for the last century, guarantees that all but a few youngsters leave our schools having really mastered the skills of reading and writing. But even today, in our largely literate society, a large number of adults of all ages have left school either unable to read or write, or with these skills only imperfectly developed. A figure of 2 million adult illiterates, or 4 per cent of the population, has been suggested, but this is based upon known cases; the true figure may well be higher.

A reading age of 9 years is the generally accepted lower limit of literacy, but this is not very satisfactory. If we consider literacy to be equated with skilled reading then a more accurate literacy level would probably be a reading age of about 12 years. This is not an unreasonable suggestion, as this level of reading ability is commonly achieved by quite large numbers of children between the ages of about 9 and 11 years. It is arguable that at reading ages below this level, reading experience will have been too limited to talk meaningfully about skilled reading. Indeed, the very term implies that the reader has had a wide variety of reading experiences.

Whilst it is not an easy task to isolate any single factor as a cause of illiteracy, or even a combination of factors for that matter, we can trace its gradual development through the school years with some degree of accuracy.

All too often it starts in the earliest stages of schooling. In the author's experience most children start school with a sense of adventure; they certainly do not start at 5 years with a sense of failure. Most of them, too, are aware that they will be expected to learn to read and write and do 'sums'. Research has shown, however, that parental emphasis in urban areas tends to be on good behaviour rather than on sound learning, and this emphasis will almost certainly affect the child's priorities and values. It is possible that what is called good behaviour may inhibit the child from asking important questions, and this could be a barrier to effective learning.

To most, if not all, 5-year-old children reading is a vague and mysterious process of which he has only a hazy idea. Where the child sees books at home, where he sees mother and father using books and has himself been introduced to them before starting school, there is a realisation of the importance of this mysterious process. There is also the added motivation of doing well in order to please both parents and teachers. The child from the non-bookish environment is therefore under a heavy handicap from the start. He struggles hard to master the intricacies of the printed word, but all too often progress is very slow. After struggling manfully through to the end of the first introductory primer, for which he may have been ill-prepared, he often finds that he has to start all over again. It is small wonder that some children throw in the towel before they leave the infant school, although more often than not they continue to go through the motions until they are about 8 or 9 years of age. Up to this age most children are still eager to please the teacher and are willing to keep on trying.

At about 9 or 10 years of age those children who have struggled with the earliest stages of reading tend to develop definite attitudes towards those subjects which depend upon book learning. If they have just about mastered the basic reading skills they consider that they can now read and do not see any necessity to develop their skills further. Those who have not mastered even the basic skills by this age tend to give up the struggle entirely. It is only a question of time before these children start to rationalise reasons why they do not need to be able to read. Very often they become trouble-makers, especially at the secondary school stage. Here the curriculum tends to be based upon the assumption that the learners can read and all too often it allows little leeway for those who cannot do so. Consequently, many of these young people drift through their secondary school careers learning little of what the system desires that they should learn and doing the minimum of work.

It is only when they leave school that realisation really dawns on these youngsters. The façade carefully erected at secondary school is quickly torn down when faced with the realities of filling in government forms for such mundane but important things as national insurance or unemployment benefits. They often have to rely on second-hand information, which may itself be inaccurate, and then it is small wonder that many of them have only a very hazy idea of what benefits they are entitled to, and equally of course, of what their responsibilities are. These people are further embarrassed when they have young children of their own whom they are unable to help with the early stages of reading. This particular problem has motivated many adult illiterates to enrol in evening classes in order to improve their limited reading ability.

In an ideal situation we should not require such classes, but there will always be some young people, quite apart from those who spend most of their school careers in special schools for slow learners, who leave school without having reached a reasonable standard of literacy. But if language and reading problems were tackled along the lines suggested in the foregoing pages then the total problem of illiteracy would not loom so large in educational thinking. This would be of benefit both to many individuals as persons and also to society as a whole.

NOTES

1  J. Taylor, *Reading and Writing in the First School* (London, Unwin Education Books, 1972).

# Appendix 1

# An Oral Reading Check List and Record Chart

Name ................................. Date of Birth......... Class/Form.........

Chronological Age ...............years ..............months

Reading Age ............years ............months Test Used ...................

| *Oral Reading Difficulties* | *Date of Reading Sessions* |
|---|---|
| Inadequate word mastery | |
| Errors on small words | |
| Insertions and omissions | |
| Inaccurate guessing | |
| Word-by-word reading | |
| Habitual repetition | |
| Inadequate phrasing | |
| Ignoring punctuation | |
| Use of finger or other aid | |
| Excessive loss of place | |
| Excessive hesitation | |
| Poor enunciation | |
| Lack of expression | |
| Tense while reading | |

Additional comments and suggestions for a remedial programme

Class/Form Teacher .......................................

(After A. J. Harris, *How to Increase Reading Ability*, New York, Longmans.)

## Appendix 2

# Specimen Case Study

Name:      Joyce H.     School: Downtown J.M.

Address:     18 Woodbine Street, Seatown

Date of Birth:  21.6.61     Position in Family: 6/6—3 boys
3 girls

*Test Results*

| Year | Details of Test | Date of Test | Results |
|------|-----------------|--------------|---------|
| | *Intelligence* | | |
| 1968/9 | Goodenough Draw-a-Man Test | 24.4.69 | C.A. 7y. 10m. M.A. 7y. 6m. Quotient 96 |
| 1968/9 | NFER Picture Test | 15.5.69 | C.A. 7y. 10m. Quotient 90 |
| 1971/2 | Raven Progressive Matrices Test | 10.7.72 | C.A. 11y. 0m. M.A. 9y. 6m. Quotient 86 |
| | *Vocabulary* | | |
| 1969/70 | English Picture Vocabulary Test | 25.5.70 | C.A. 8y. 11m. Standarised Score 80 Percentile 9 |
| 1971/2 | Crichton Vocabulary Scale | 10.7.72 | C.A. 11y. 0m. M.A. 7y. 0m. Quotient 67 |
| | *Reading* | | |
| 1968 | Vernon Word Recognition | 29.4.69 | C.A. 7y 10m. No Score |
| 1970/1 | Schonell R3A | 21.1.71 | C.A. 9y. 7m. R.A. 6y. 10m. Reading Quotient 71 |

1971/2   Neale Analysis of Reading Ability   10.7.72   C.A. 11y. 0m.
R.A.
Rate 9y. 2m.
Accuracy
9y. 1m.
Comprehen-
sion 8y. 10m.
Reading
Quotient 82

1971/2   Vernon Word Recognition Test   17.7.72   C.A.2 11y. 0m.
R.A. 8y. 9m.
Reading
Quotient 80

## Health Record

| | | |
|---|---|---|
| (a) | General health — | good. No serious illness apart from the usual children's illnesses in the infant school. |
| (b) | Eyesight — | normal. |
| (c) | Hearing — | normal, although Joyce seems to suffer from perpetual catarrhal infections which might possibly cause some hearing loss at intervals. |

## School Attendance

| Year | Possible | Actual | Comments |
|---|---|---|---|
| 1966/7 | 380 | 350 | Measles and mumps were the cause of absence. |
| 1967/8 | 382 | 345 | Chickenpox and colds were the reasons for absence in three longish spells. |
| 1968/9 | 380 | 360 | Odd days off for colds. |
| 1969/70 | 380 | 365 | One or two days off for colds and for helping mother who has had a bad year for illness. |
| 1970/1 | 382 | 370 | |
| 1971/2 | 380 | | |

### General Comments

Joyce dislikes having time off. In fact she has often attended school when she should have been at home in bed. Very occasionally she has to help out at home when her mother is ill, but Joyce's record in this respect is better than that of many other children.

*School Attainment*

1970/1    It is difficult to assess Joyce's true attainment. She is very quiet and reserved in the classroom and does not talk easily. (From what one gathers this behaviour does not apply at home.) Her test results indicate that she has only limited ability, but nevertheless she should be able to do rather better than her present classroom performance. She tries very hard with all her school work, but her withdrawn personality probably limits the development of her full potential. One would have a much better idea of Joyce's difficulties if she would be more forthcoming in both answering and asking questions.

*Mathematics.* Joyce enjoys doing 'sums', but because of her limited ability in reading she is not happy with problem work. She has quite a good grasp of number relationships, but her knowledge of mathematical concepts is limited.

*Language work.* Joyce's achievements in this area are limited by her lack of reading ability and her reluctance to speak in oral language work. In the last few months, February to May 1971, she has made some progress and seems to be taking much more interest in certain aspects of English, especially spelling. She has also started to keep a diary in which she shows considerable interest.

*Topic work.* Again limited reading ability hinders achievement. Joyce shows interest in many aspects of topic work, but any tasks which she is set have to be clearly defined and not too difficult.

*Art.* Although she does not profess great interest in this aspect of the curriculum Joyce nevertheless produces some very interesting work in art. Her sense of colour and spatial relationships seem to be quite well developed.

*PE and games.* Joyce shows little interest in any aspect except swimming at which she has some ability.

Joyce's parents show a limited interest in her work. They are certainly not uninterested, but they do not seem quite certain just how active they should be or what steps to take to support the work of the school in the home situation.

*Interests*

1970/1    Joyce does not seem to be a lonely child. She claims to have many friends at home and is certainly not an isolate in the class group.

Most evenings she enjoys playing 'tag' on the street with her friends, but she has to be in by 7.00 p.m. The rest of the time is spent watching television. Her favourite programmes are *Tom and Jerry Cartoons* and the *Fantastic Four*, a children's series shown on the ITV network.

Indoor games are limited, but for Christmas Joyce got *Monopoly* and *Cluedo* and now spends some time each week playing one of these games with some of her brothers and sisters who are still at school.

As is the case with most childen in the school, if not in the area, Joyce has no interest or activity which one would classify as a hobby.

Again as is the case with many children in the school Joyce has few books of her own at home, those she does possess are mainly of the comic annual variety bought at Christmas. She is not a member of the public library, which is hardly surprising in view of her limited reading ability. Indeed reading seems to be an activity only indulged in at school.

## Reading Ability

### (a) The basic skills

*Basic Reader – Royal Road Readers Book 1*

1968/9   Joyce has had considerable difficulty with reading throughout the infant school and despite extra teaching she is still not familiar with the basic skills. Although she is now starting to read the basic primers with some degree of fluency she needs systematic practice in phonic skills and a programme of reading experience to develop word attack skills. Joyce can cope with words in context with a reasonable degree of facility, but makes no attempt to tackle new words in isolation.

1970/1   Joyce is now making some progress. Her mastery of the basic skills, although still not good, has improved and she is able to tackle new words with greater confidence. She works very hard and is keen to improve her reading. Although she still needs practice at reading aloud, she is able to read short passages silently. These are gradually being made longer as progress is made.

1971/2   As the test results indicate, Joyce has made considerable progress. Her mastery of the basic skills is much improved, she has much more self-confidence and she has started to explore a wider range of reading experiences. She is now reading 'Secret Seven' stories by Enid Blyton with considerable pleasure and enjoyment.

### (b) Comprehension skills

1968/9   Although she only reads with difficulty Joyce seems to have a fair understanding of what she has read. She likes story books and was highly critical of some reading books because they did not contain any stories. Her knowledge of the concept 'story' is quite well developed for a child with such limited ability, for instance she has a good grasp of both characters and plot of her favourite story 'Goldilocks and the Three Bears' and of some other fairly tales which she enjoys.

1970/1   Joyce's reading has improved to such an extent that it is possible to measure her skill in certain aspects of comprehension, note, for example, the score on the Schonell R3A test. But her rate of reading is still too slow and laboured for her to remember much more than is contained in a page of text. If she is told a story she can remember quite a lot of detail about it.

1971/2 Joyce is now able to read a story and grasp the essential details of it, although she still has difficulty with specialised texts, for instance mathematics text books or work cards. In such subjects one has to limit the amount of reading and ensure that the text is clear and the problem well defined for her.

### Diagnosis and Treatment

#### [1968/9]

*Diagnosis.* Weaknesses arising from slow development of reading and difficulty in mastering the basic skills, notably word attack and phonic skills.

*Treatment* (a) Change to Royal Road reading scheme.
          (b) Regular practice with the Stott Programmed Reading Kit.
          (c) Simple word puzzles and games, including *Junior Scrabble.*
          (d) Use of oral language to widen reading experiences.

*Evaluation.* Joyce has worked with enthusiasm and there are definite signs of improvement. She is tackling reading with greater confidence and is not giving up easily when she meets new words in a text. She now adopts a systematic strategy for attacking new words. Joyce can tell a story in her own words orally and if helped with the writing is able to read it back with some degree of fluency. She is building up an interesting booklet of her own stories which she enjoys reading and of which she is quite proud.

#### [1970/1]

*Diagnosis.* Although mastery of the basic skills has improved, there are weaknesses in comprehension, even at a very simple level. She does not read quickly enough to remember much more than a page from a reading book.

*Treatment.* (1) The use of comprehension work cards devised by the teacher to develop literal comprehension skills of the most basic kind:
(a) Cards containing short straightforward stories with questions on characters, plot and sequence.
(b) Simple task cards requiring the reader to locate information and/or to follow explicit instructions.
(2) Practice in timed reading of selected passages to encourage faster reading. The teacher checks understanding by asking questions on the passage.

*Evaluation.* The programme seems to have met with some success. The task cards could have been more carefully graded in the early stages when too much was attempted too early. Once this was recognised and the cards were more vigorously graded, progress improved. This comment applies particularly to those task cards which were related to work in mathematics or topics, for instance in environmental studies.

Joyce is now really enjoying her reading and tackles it with enthusiasm, but if she is to make further progress she should continue with a planned reading programme which will help her to develop comprehension skills of a higher order over a wide range of reading experiences.

Regular practice with one of the easier reading laboratories might be a useful adjunct to learning.

## NOTES

J. C. Daniels and H. Diack, *Royal Road Readers* (Chatto & Windus, 1956).
D. H. Stott, *Programmed Reading Kit* (Holmes, 1962).

The author hopes that readers will forgive any inaccuracies and inadequacies in this case study. It is based upon a number of case studies from the author's own research and upon his experience in the classroom.

Ideally, entries should be made regularly at weekly or monthly intervals, but it was not possible to give so much detail in this example. Instead, the author has summarised the comments into an annual report, which has only limited value as it covers too great a time span. Remedial programmes must be evaluated at regular intervals in order to assess their effectiveness and for this purpose even a term might be too long.

Such case studies would only be made in exceptional cases such as that of Joyce. (The author is well aware that there is not the time to keep such full and detailed records for all children in the course of a normal teaching day.) Thus while the report may seem lengthy, it is necessary to analyse and diagnose as accurately as possible the problems of children like Joyce if they are to be given the maximum possible assistance. Individual teachers have to see what has already been done, what progress, if any, has been made and what still needs to be done. All too often time is lost in this part of the procedure and for the child time is valuable; it is certainly not on his side in the race to catch up with his more fortunate fellows. No effort should be too great to give these children all the help they need.

## Appendix 3

# Some Useful Reading Series for Slow Readers

| Title | Publisher | Reading Grade Level | Interest Grade Level |
|---|---|---|---|
| CHECKERED FLAG SERIES | San Francisco, Field | 2 | 6–11 |
| ENCOUNTERS: REALITY IN READING AND LANGUAGE SERIES | New York, Cambridge Book | 1–5 | up to 7 |
| GATEWAY BOOKS | New York, Random House | 2–3 | 3–9 |
| THE INTERESTING READING SERIES | Chicago, Follett | 2–3 | 4–11 |
| SPACE AGE BOOKS | Westchester, Ill., Benefic | 2–3 | 2–6 |
| ALL ABOUT BOOKS SERIES | Chicago, Children's Press | 2–4 | 2–8 |
| THE DEEP SEA ADVENTURE SERIES | San Francisco, Field | 2–4 | 3–9 |
| DISCOVERY BOOKS | Champaign, Ill., Garrard | 2–4 | 3–6 |
| JUNIOR EVERYREADERS | Manchester, Mo., Webster | 2–4 | 2–7 |
| THE MORGAN BAY SERIES | San Francisco, Field | 2–4 | 4–9 |
| THE WILDLIFE ADVENTURE SERIES | San Francisco, Field | 2–4 | 3–8 |
| THE WORLD OF ADVENTURE SERIES | Westchester, Ill., Benefic | 2–5 | 3–9 |
| AMERICAN ADVENTURE SERIES | New York, Harper & Row | 2–6 | 4–9 |
| FOLKLORE OF THE WORLD BOOKS | Champaign, Ill., Garrard | 3 | 2–8 |
| MORGAN BAY MYSTERIES | San Francisco, Field | 3–4 | 3–8 |
| JUNIOR SCIENCE BOOKS | Champaign, Ill., Garrard | 3–4 | 3–6 |
| THE FIRST BOOKS | New York, Watts | 3–5 | 3–8 |
| EVERY READER LIBRARY | Manchester, Mo., Webster | 4–5 | 4–10 |
| CHILDHOOD OF FAMOUS AMERICANS SERIES | Indianapolis, Bobbs-Merrill | 4–5 | 4–9 |
| TEEN AGE TALES | Boston, Heath | 4–6 | 6–11 |
| SIMPLIFIED CLASSICS | New York, Scott | 4–5 | 4–10 |
| WE WERE THERE BOOKS | Eau Claire, Wis., Hale | 4–5 | 5–9 |
| ALLABOUT BOOKS | New York, Random House | 4–6 | 5–11 |
| MODERN ADVENTURE STORIES | New York, Harper & Row | 4–6 | 4–11 |
| RELUCTANT READER LIBRARY | New York, Scholastic | 4–7 | up to 12 |
| LANDMARK BOOKS | New York, Random House | 5–7 | 5–11 |

## Appendix 4

# Useful Booklets for Guidance in the Selection of Reading Materials

Dunn, Anita E. and Mabel E. Jackman. *Fare for the Reluctant Reader*, 3rd ed. Albany, N. Y.: Capital Area Achool Development Association, State University of New York at Albany, 1964.

Harris, Albert J. and Edward R. Sipay. *How to Increase Reading Ability: A Guide to Developmental and Remedial Methods*, 6th ed. New York: McKay, 1975.

Roswell, Florence G. and Gladys Natchez. *Reading Disability: Diagnosis and Treatment*, 2nd rev. ed. New York: Basic Books, 1971.

Spache, George D. *Good Reading for Poor Readers*, rev. ed. Champaign, Ill.: Garrard, 1974

## Appendix 5

# Tests of Reading Attainment and Diagnostic Tests

Group Tests

CALIFORNIA READING TESTS. Monterey, Calif.: California Test Bureau, Division of McGraw-Hill. (grades 1–2; 3–lower 4; 4–6; 7–9; 9–college)
DAVIS READING TEST. New York: Psychological Corp. (grades 8–11; 11–13)
McCULLOUGH WORD ANALYSIS TESTS. Waltham, Mass.: Ginn. (grades 4–8)
METROPOLITAN ACHIEVEMENT TESTS. New York: Harcourt Brace Jovanovich. (five levels—grades 1; 2–3.5; 3–4; 5–6; 7–8)
SEQUENTIAL TESTS OF EDUCATIONAL PROGRESS: READING. Princeton, N. J.: Educational Testing Service. (Level 4, grades 4–6; Level 3, grades 7–9; Level 2, grades 10–12)
SRA ACHIEVEMENT SERIES: READING. Chicago: Science Research Associates. (grades 1–9)

Individual and Diagnostic Tests

BASIC SIGHT WORD TEST. Champaign, Ill.: Garrard. (grades 1–2)
DURRELL ANALYSIS OF READING DIFFICULTY. New York: Harcourt Brace Jovanovich.
GILMORE ORAL READING TEST. New York: Harcourt Brace Jovanovich. (grades 1–8)
GRAY ORAL READING TEST. Indianapolis: Bobbs-Merrill. (grades 1–10)
ROSWELL-CHALL DIAGNOSTIC READING TEST: ANALYZING PHONIC KNOWLEDGE AND SKILLS. New York: Essay Press.
STAMFORD DIAGNOSTIC READING TEST. New York: Harcourt Brace Jovanovich. (Level I, grades 2.5–4.5; Level II, grades 4.5–8.5)
SPACHE DIAGNOSTIC READING SCALES. Monterey, Calif.: California Test Bureau, Division of McGraw-Hill. (grades 1 and up)
WIDE RANGE ACHIEVEMENT TEST: READING, SPELLING, ARITHMETIC FROM KINDERGARTEN TO COLLEGE. New York: Psychological Corp. (age 5 to adult)

# Bibliography

Ablewhite, R. *The Slow Reader* (London, Heinemann, 1967)

Adams, P. (ed.) *Language in Thinking* (Harmondsworth, Penguin, 1972)

Bartlett, F. C. 'The Measurement of Human Skill', in *British Medical Journal* (London, British Medical Association, 1947), Nos. 4510, 4511

Bernstein, B. *Class, Codes and Control* (New York, Schocken, 1975)

Brandis, W. and Henderson, D. *Social Class, Language and Communication* (London, Routledge, 1970)

Burt, C. *The Backward Child* (London, University of London Press, 1937)

Chambers, A. *The Reluctant Reader* (Oxford, Pergamon Press, 1969)

Chomsky, N. *Aspects of the Theory of Syntax* (Cambridge, Mass., MIT Press, 1965)

Clark, M. M. *Reading Difficulties in Schools* (Harmondsworth, Penguin, 1970)

Clegg, A. B. *The Excitement of Writing* (New York, Schocken, 1972)

Cox, M. *The Challenge of Reading Failure* (Slough, NFER, 1968)

Crawford, A. Unpublished manuscript of research undertaken into the incidence of reading failure at junior school level in Liverpool (Liverpool, 1966)

Creber, J. W. P. *Lost for Words* (Harmondsworth, Penguin, 1972)

Dale, E. and Chall, J. S. 'A Formula for Predicting Readability', in *Educational Research Bulletin*, No. 27 (1948)

Davie, R., Butler, N. and Goldstein, H. *From Birth to Seven* (London, Longmans, 1972)

De Cecco, J. P. (ed.) *The Psychology of Language, Thought and Instruction* (New York, Holt, Rinehart & Winston, 1967)

Department of Education and Science. *Children and their Primary Schools: The Plowden Report* (London, HMSO, 1967), Vols 1 and 2

Douglas, J. W. B. *The Home and the School* (London, MacGibbon & Kee, 1964)

Downing, J. 'How Children Think about Reading', Distinguished Leader's Address to IRA (Kansas City, 1969), unpublished

Durrell, D. D. *Improving Reading Instruction* (New York, Harcourt, Brace & World, 1956)

Fries, C. C. *Linguistics and Reading* (New York, Holt, Rinehart & Winston, 1963)

Gagné, R. M. *The Conditions of Learning* (New York, Holt, Rinehart & Winston, 1970)

Gardner, W. K. *Towards Literacy* (Oxford, Blackwell, 1965)

Giglioli, P. P. (ed.). *Language and Social Context* (Harmondsworth, Penguin, 1972)

Gilliland, J. *Readability* (London, University of London Press, 1972)

Ginsberg, H. *The Myth of the Deprived Child* (New Jersey, Prentice-Hall, 1972)

Harris, A. J. *How to Increase Reading Ability* (New York, Longmans, 1970), 5th edn

Herriot, P. *An Introduction to the Psychology of Language* (London, Methuen, 1970)
  *Language and Teaching* (London, Methuen, 1971)

Jeffreys, M. V. C. *Personal Values in the Modern World* (London, Penguin, 1960)

Kellmer Pringle, M. L., Butler, N. R. and Davie, R. *11,000 Seven-Year-Olds* (London, Longmans, 1966)

Kozol, J. *Death at an Early Age* (Harmondsworth, Penguin, 1967)

Lefevre, C. A. *Linguistics and the Teaching of Reading* (Chicago, Chicago Teachers' College, 1962)

Lewis, M. M. *Language and the Child* (Slough, NFER, 1969)

Lovell, K. and Woolsey, M. E. 'Reading Disability, Non-Verbal Reasoning and Social Class' (in *Educational Research*), Vol. 6 (1964)

Lunzer, E. A. and Morris J. E. (eds.). *Development in Human Learning* (London, Staples Press, 1968), Vol. 2.

Luria, A. R. and Yudovich, F. La. *Speech and the Development of Mental Processes in the Child* (London, Penguin, 1956)

McLuhan, M. *The Gutenberg Galaxy* (London, Routledge, 1962)

Mead, M. 'Our Educational Emphasis in Primitive Perspective', in *American Journal of Sociology* (Chicago, University of Chicago Press, 1946), Vol. 48

Melnik, A. and Merritt, J. (eds.). *Reading Today and Tomorrow* (London, University of London Press for the Open University, 1972)
  *The Reading Curriculum* (London, University of London Press, 1972)

Morris, J. M. *Standards and Progress in Reading* (Slough, NFER, 1966)

Morris, R. *Success and Failure in Learning to Read* (Harmondsworth, Penguin, 1972)

Moyle, D. *The Teaching of Reading* (London, Ward Lock Educational, 1968)

Moyle, D. and Moyle, L. M. *Modern Innovations in the Teaching of Reading* (London, University of London Press, 1970)

Open University. *Language in Education* (London, Routledge & Kegan Paul, 1972)

Opie, I. and Opie, P. *The Lore and Language of Schoolchildren* (London, Oxford University Press, 1959)

Phillpotts, B. *Edda and Saga* (London, Butterworth, 1931)

Piaget, J. *Language and Thought of the Child* (London, Routledge, 1923)

Ravenette, A. T. *Dimensions of Reading Difficulties* (Oxford, Pergamon Press, 1968)

Reid, J. F. 'Learning to Think about Reading', in *Educational Research*, Vol. 9 (Slough, NFER, November 1966)

(ed.). *Reading: Problems and Practices* (London, Ward Lock Educational, 1972)

Roberts, G. R. *Reading in Primary Schools* (London, Routledge, 1969)
*Early Reading Skills in UKRA Reading Skills* (London, Ward Lock Educational, 1970)

Robinson, H. A. (ed.). *Meeting Individual Differences in Reading* (Chicago, Chicago University Press, 1964)

Rosenthal, R. and Jacobson, L. F. *Pygmalion in the Classroom* (New York, Holt, Rinehart & Winston, 1968)

Roswell, F. and Natchez, G. *Reading Disability, Diagnosis and Treatment* (New York, Basic Books, 1964)

Saporta, S. (ed.). *Psycho-linguistics* (New York, Holt, Rinehart & Winston, 1961)

Schonell, F. J. *The Psychology and Teaching of Reading* (Edinburgh, Oliver & Boyd, 1945)

School of Barbiana, *Letter to a Teacher* (Harmondsworth, Penguin, 1970)

Start, K. B. and Wells, B. K. *The Trend of Reading Standards* (Slough, NFER, 1972)

Stott, D. H. *Roads to Literacy* (London, Holmes, 1964)

Tansley, A. E. *Reading and Remedial Reading* (London, Routledge, 1967)

Taylor, J. *Reading and Writing in the First School* (London, Unwin Education Books, 1973)

Taylor, W. L. 'Cloze Procedure: A New Tool for Measuring Readability' (in *Journalism Quarterly*), Vol. 30

Tough, J. *Talking, Thinking, Growing* (New York, Schocken, 1974)

Vygotsky, L. S. *Thought and Language* (Cambridge, Mass., MIT Press, 1962)

Watts, A. F. *The Language and Mental Development of Children* (London, Harrap, 1944)

Wilkinson, A. M. *Spoken English*, Educational Review Occasional Publications (Birmingham, University of Birmingham Press, 1965)
*The Foundations of Language* (London, Oxford University Press, 1971)

Wiseman, S. *Education and Environment* (Manchester, Manchester University Press, 1964)

# Index